TRUE EDUCATION READER

SILENT, ORAL, MEMORY

THIRD GRADE—PART ONE

By
SARAH ELIZABETH PECK

Published for the Department of Education of the
General Conference of Seventh-day Adventists

"So they read in the Book
In the law of God
Distinctly,
And gave the sense, and
Caused them to understand
The reading."
—*Bible (Nehemiah 8:8).*

TEACH Services, Inc.
PUBLISHING
www.TEACHServices.com • (800) 367-1844

World rights reserved. This book or any portion thereof may not be copied or reproduced in any form or manner whatever, except as provided by law, without the written permission of the publisher, except by a reviewer who may quote brief passages in a review.

The author assumes full responsibility for the accuracy of all facts and quotations as cited in this book. The opinions expressed in this book are the author's personal views and interpretations, and do not necessarily reflect those of the publisher.

This book is provided with the understanding that the publisher is not engaged in giving spiritual, legal, medical, or other professional advice. If authoritative advice is needed, the reader should seek the counsel of a competent professional.

Copyright © 2005 TEACH Services, Inc.
ISBNN-13: 978-1-57258-345-0 (Paperback)
Library of Congress Control Number: 2005903152

Acknowledgments

For permission to reprint copyrighted material grateful acknowledgment is made as follows:

To Frederick A. Stokes Company, for the reprint of "The Snow Baby."

To Charles Scribner's Sons, for poems by Robert Louis Stevenson.

To D. C. Heath & Company, for "The Tree Frog" and "Joe Black" from the "Gordon Third Reader."

Poems by Frank Dempster Sherman are used by permission of, and arrangement with, Houghton, Mifflin Company.

INTRODUCTION

Basic Principles of Reading

Reading is the key that unlocks the door to knowledge. Until children can get thought accurately and quickly from the printed page, they are handicapped in their progress in arithmetic, in language, and in every content subject.

But reading is more than the key to *knowledge*. It is a key to *character*. Nothing is more vitally important than the molding of the pupil's taste for that which is good and pure and true and noble. And in accomplishing this, reading is one of the most potent factors. To create in the child's own heart a distaste for the cheap, the trifling, the untrue, in language and thought, so that he voluntarily rejects all these and *chooses* that which is uplifting—this is the great goal of the teacher of reading. This is real character building.

To the boy or girl in training to be a missionary for God, reading is also a key to *soul winning,* for through reading he may open before others eternal truth. If the truth of God is presented in language that is distinct and clear, people will listen with pleasure. If it is given in tones that convey the depth of beautiful meaning, whether it be warning, sympathy, appeal, or love, the intelligence will be convinced, and the soul may be won to obedience.

This is the way Jesus read. When He stood up in the synagogue on the Sabbath day to read, He reached the very soul of His hearers. He read with such fullness of meaning in His voice that when He sat down "the eyes of all them that were in the synagogue were fastened on Him." They "wondered at the gracious words which proceeded out of His mouth." Such reading will prepare our boys and girls to be witnesses for Him.

In an endeavor to aid the teacher in placing these keys in the hands of our boys and girls, and also to give the children a balanced reading diet, the lessons in this book cover a wide range. A list of the reading projects is found under "Contents by Projects" in the Teachers' Edition. In this list are found the Bible, the great source book of all that makes reading worth while; nature, God's other book; experiences from the lives of men and women who have made God's word the guide of their actions; the noble deeds of missionaries who have followed their Lord in consecrating their best and their all to helping their needy brothers; the inspiration of those who through toil and perseverance have given up ease and personal pleasure in order to bequeath to the world their best in literature, in art, in music, in invention, in discovery—these are some of the sources that have been appealed to in the preparation of these lessons in reading for our growing boys and girls, the boys and girls who "if rightly trained" are to take an active part in finishing God's work in the earth in this generation.

In revising this series of school readers it has not been found necessary to draw from the unreal and purely imaginative. The books are therefore entirely free from myths, fairy tales, and all that tends to undermine faith in the Sacred Word, and to unfit the pupil for the highest service. Many conscientious educators and parents recognize the constantly increasing tendency in the world to-day toward a lack of faith in God and His word, which is but the natural result of much of the teaching of the present age. Many school readers abound with that which is false and fanciful, and this cannot but do much to unfit the mind to meet the realities of life and to appreciate sober truth. To help stem this tide toward the artificial and the skeptical, the subject matter in these readers is drawn entirely from the true and the beautiful in life, in nature, and in revelation. The author believes that "truth is stranger than fiction," fact more wonderful than fancy; and that the imagination of the child can therefore be best aroused, interested, and developed in the realm of truth and fact.

Such thoughts nourishing the minds of the young day after day and year after year will mold their lives and do much in winning them for "the joy of service in this world, and for the higher joy of wider service in the world to come."

CONTENTS

In this Table of Contents, S or O following a title indicates whether the lesson is best fitted for silent or for oral reading. Readings marked S with a number following, as S1, S2, etc., are for special silent reading drills or practice tests, the results of which may be recorded on the "Graph of Pupil's Weekly Silent Reading Rate," in the back of the reader. The number following the titles of certain poems is the number of words the poem contains.

FIRST PERIOD

	PAGE
LEARNING TO READ	1
MEMORIZING THE SCRIPTURES S1	5
THE SHEPHERD PSALM 117 .... *King David*	8
HOW TO READ QUICKLY	9
THE SPIDER S	10
UNCLE PHIL'S STORY S	13
THE DOG WITH A LANTERN S	16
HERO AND JET S2	18
ORAL READING	21
THE ECHO O	24
ROBERT LOUIS STEVENSON S	25
BED IN SUMMER 87 .... *Robert Louis Stevenson*	33
MEMORY READING	34
BEDTIME 58	37
A MOTHER'S SONG 65	38
LITTLE "JOHN PETER" S	39
THE TREE FROG S3 .... *Gordon Third Reader*	45
THE SUN'S TRAVELS 77 .... *Robert Louis Stevenson*	48
THE CLOUD 88	50
BABYLAND 97 .... *George Cooper*	51
THE MT. RORAIMA CHURCH SCHOOL S	52
TAUGHT BY A PARROT O	57
A SPELLING STAIRWAY S4	58
SIGNBOARDS TO HEALTHLAND S	60
TINY'S ALARM CLOCK O .... *Christian Advocate*	61
LITTLE PAPOOSE LULLABY 78 .... *Charles Myall*	64

COLUMBUS AND A NEW WORLD ^S	66
AN AX TO GRIND ^{S5}	73
PAYING TOO MUCH FOR A WHISTLE ^{S5}	76
READING TESTS AND SCORES FOR THE FIRST PERIOD	79

SECOND PERIOD

THE LITTLE DICTIONARY TEACHER		80
READING DRILLS FOR THE SECOND PERIOD		82
POLITE AWAY FROM HOME ^O	*Pansy*	83
PROVERBS OF SOLOMON ^O	*The Bible*	86
"GIVE US THIS DAY OUR DAILY BREAD" ^S		87
THE PRAYER OF A POOR WOMAN ^S		90
TOWSER AND THE CHICKS ^{S1}	*Christian Work*	92
DAISIES ⁸⁰	*Frank Dempster Sherman*	96
CLOUDS ¹³⁹	*Frank Dempster Sherman*	97
THE FLY ^O		98
HALF AN APPLE ^O		100
OLD TUSKY ^S		104
DIAMOND ^{S2}		110
MARY'S LAMB ^O	*Sarah J. Hale*	115
THE RAINDROPS' JOURNEY ⁸³		116
A LITTLE GIRL WHOM GOD USED ^S		117
JOE BLACK ^{S3}	*Gordon Third Reader*	124
OBEDIENCE ⁴²	*Phœbe Cary*	127
WHAT TO LOOK FOR ⁵²	*Alice Cary*	127
ROBERT BRUCE AND THE SPIDER ^S		128
TIMOUR AND THE ANT ^S		131
GRACE DARLING ^S		132
A FAWN SAVED FROM DOGS ^{S4}	*Youth's Instructor*	139
THE BOY AND HIS CAP ¹⁰⁴	*Rebecca B. Foresman*	141
MY SHADOW ¹⁸⁸	*Robert Louis Stevenson*	142
IN A MINUTE ^O	*Youth's Instructor*	144
A LITTLE GENTLEMAN ^O		146
A BOX OF PEARLS ^S		148
PENN'S TREATY WITH THE INDIANS ^S		153
DID BOB THINK? ^{S5}		159
WHAT TO BE ^O	*The Independent*	161
PETER PAUL AUGUSTUS ^O		162
GRANDPAPA'S SPECTACLES ^O	*Elizabeth Sill*	163
READING TESTS AND SCORES FOR THE SECOND PERIOD		165

THIRD PERIOD

READING DRILLS FOR THE THIRD PERIOD 166
EVEN THE WINDS OBEY HIM [S] 167
PRETTY POLLY [O] 169
FLY-AWAY [O] 172
A TWO-THOUSAND DOLLAR
   MOUSE HOUSE [S1] .... *Youth's Instructor* 174
THE ANT AND THE CRICKET [O] ..... *Frances Jenkins Olcott* .. 177
RATU MELI, A NATIVE CHIEF OF FIJI [S] 178
THE WEATHER [101] .... *Nancy Byrd Turner* 184
MY CHICKADEE GUESTS [S] .... *Ernest Harold Baynes* ... 185
NAOMI [S2] 191
DON'T GIVE UP [87] .... *Phœbe Cary* 195
TO A HONEYBEE [82] .... *Alice Cary* 196
STORIES OF LINCOLN [O] .... *"True Stories of Lincoln"* 197
WASHINGTON'S LOVE FOR CHILDREN [S] 200
A LITTLE SLAVE'S FAITH [S3] 202
THE CHURN THAT WAS NEVER
   THROUGH CHURNING [S] .... *Arthur W. Spalding* 204
THE ILL-NATURED BRIER [O] .... *Anna Bache* 211
LITTLE "SCOTCH GRANITE" [O] ..... *Sunday School Visitor* ... 213
BRUNO [S4] .... *Jacob Abbott* 217
HOW THE STREET SWEEPER BECAME A MINISTER [O] 221
ROSA BONHEUR [S] 224
LITTLE FOXES [135] .... *Sunshine and Shadow* ... 230
WHAT THE MINUTES SAY [113] 232
THE SNOW BABY [S5] .... *"The Snow Baby"* 233
MOTHER'S BOY [O] .... *The Sabbath Recorder* ... 239
MOTHER'S GIRL [O] 240
READING TESTS AND SCORES FOR THE THIRD PERIOD 242
THE LITTLE DICTIONARY TEACHER 243
MAPS .... X, XI, XII
GRAPHS OF PUPIL'S WEEKLY SILENT READING RATE 252

Map of the New World

Map of the Old World

Map of the United States

Learning to Read[1]

To the Boys and Girls in the Third Grade:

You are now beginning your third year in school. This is a very im·por′tant year in your ed·u·ca′tion. You are one year older than you were last year, and you should be able to do more work than you did then.

In reading, you will learn to read more easily and more quickly than you did in the second grade. So you will be able to read more nice little books. Won't that be fine!

Your new reader is full of in′ter·est·ing stories. There are stories about dogs, and birds, and horses, and elephants, and other animals. There are stories about children who have had the same temp·ta′tions that you have, and how they learned to do right.

---

[1] TO THE TEACHER: Before teaching any of the lessons in this book, read carefully what is said in the "Introduction" and "To the Teacher" in the section "Reading, Grades Three and Four" of the "Teacher's Handbook on the Elementary Curriculum." "Learning to Read" may be read to the class or given orally by the teacher to the pupils. Or the pupils may read it silently before class time. It is designed to suggest how the year's work in reading may be introduced. Read also in "Reading Tests and Scores for Third Grade" how to find and record the reading rate and comprehension of each pupil.

There are other stories about children who live in far-away lands.

There are some stories about great men and women who loved children. As you read about these men and women, you will learn to love them. Some of them have written beautiful poems for children, and you will enjoy reading these poems.

Best of all, there are some wonderfully interesting stories about missions and mis′sion-a-ries, and how God is working for them. There are *many more* stories than you had in your little second reader, and some of them are longer. But *third* grade children can read them *easily!*

When you were in the second grade, you learned to read silently from 60 to 80 words a minute. By the time you finish the third grade, you should be able to read about 100 words a minute! Think of *that!*

To-day, we are going to see how much you can read in one minute. I am wondering who can read 80 words right at the very beginning of this year. Of course, you must *think* about what you are reading, and *understand* what it *means*, or else it won't count at all.

Turn to page five in your reader. Here is a story named "Mem′o-riz-ing the Scrip′tures." There are two words in this story that I want to be sure you know before you begin to read so you won't have to stop and wonder what they are. These words are am′bu-lance and hos′pi-tal. Do you know what an ambulance is? I am sure you have heard of a hospital. Look at these words carefully, and let us say them together. Then you will know them when you read them in the story.

This story tells about a little boy who was run over one day in a big city. It tells what a good man did for the poor little boy to make him feel better. As you read, find out who the little boy was, what ran over him, and what the good man did to help him bear his suffering. Find out, also, if you can, what good lesson we may learn from this story.

When you have read for three minutes, the teacher will say, "Mark!" Just as soon as she speaks, you may make a light pencil dot after the word you are then reading, and go right on reading till you finish the story.

What are you to do when your teacher says, "Mark"?

What are you to do after you make the mark?

Ready! Point with your pencil to the first word in the story. Then, all eyes on the teacher!

Read!

PLOCKHORST. 1825.

"The Good Shepherd"

THIRD GRADE—PART ONE
FIRST PERIOD

Memorizing the Scriptures [S1]

"Mother, I don't see why you have me learn a psalm every month," said Eva Preston. "None of the other girls do, and one can always *read* them."

Her mother said nothing for a moment. "You don't see the use of learning them now, dear," she then said gently, "but you will when you are a little older."

The next day was Sabbath. A stranger talked to the Sabbath school.

"I work among the poor children in a big city," he said. "Many of these children sell newspapers. They are my little friends. One day, one of them, whose name was Joe, was run over by a horse and wagon. He was carried to a drug store near by to wait for the ambulance to take him to the hospital. The doctor and I were with him, and a crowd was in the store. The boy suffered terribly, but he was a brave little fellow. All at once, he said, 'If I could hear about the Shepherd, I could bear it better.'

"I knew what he meant, for at the mission school I had told them about King David's beautiful shepherd psalm. I said it now, over and over, and I wish you could have seen the look in his face as he listened. That little rough newsboy said after me, 'And I will dwell in the house of the Lord forever.' Before the ambulance came, Joe was dead.

"I tell you this, dear children, because few of us learn scriptures by heart. We think it is not im-por'tant. But I know it is. I wonder, now, if any child can re-peat' the twenty-third psalm for me."

There was a long pause. No one stirred. Then Eva Preston stood up and re-peat'ed it very clearly and cor-rect'ly.

"Thank you, my dear," the min'is-ter said to Eva, as she finished. "You have a gift that no one can take from you."

Reading Rate and Comprehension

How many words did you read a minute? This is called your *reading rate*. Your teacher will show you how to mark your rate on your rate graph in the back of your reader.

You may now *write* answers to the ten questions below. Use only one or two words for each answer. If you can answer all the questions correctly, it will show that you have really *read* the story, and not just hurried over the words. The number of questions answered will show your grade in *com-pre-hen′sion*, or understanding what you read.

Comprehension Test

1. What was the little boy's name?
2. What work did he do in the city?
3. Did a street car run over him one day?
4. Was he taken to the hospital for help?
5. Was he afraid to die?
6. Whom did he ask to hear about?
7. What psalm did the good man repeat to him?
8. Where did the good man tell this story?
9. Who repeated this psalm in Sabbath school?
10. Do you think this story helped Eva to see the use of memorizing scriptures?

If you answered seven questions correctly, your comprehension grade is 70. If you answered eight questions correctly, it is 80. What is it if you answer 5 questions? 10 questions? What *was* your comprehension grade?

The Shepherd Psalm [117]

The Lord is my Shepherd; I shall not want.
He maketh me to lie down
    in green pas′tures:
He leadeth me beside the still waters.

He re-stor′eth my soul:
He leadeth me in the paths of righteousness
For His name's sake.

Yea, though I walk through the valley
    of the shadow of death,
I will fear no evil: for Thou art with me;
Thy rod and Thy staff they comfort me.

Thou pre-par′est a table before me
In the pres′ence of mine enemies:
Thou a-noint′est my head with oil;
My cup runneth over.

Surely goodness and mer′cy shall follow me
    all the days of my life:
And I will dwell in the house of the Lord
    forever.

— *King David.*

Which psalm is called, "The Shepherd Psalm"?
Who wrote this psalm? Find it in your Bible.

The Shepherd Psalm is one of the most beautiful psalms in the Bible. Every one should know it. Can you repeat it clearly and correctly, as Eva did?

How to Read Quickly

One of the first things to do in learning to read quickly is to be able to see a number of words at once, just as when you were in the first grade you learned to see at one glance all the *letters* that make up a *word*. When you see the word *spider*, you do not have to think of each letter, s-p-i-d-e-r, before you know the word, do you? In just this way, when you see several *words* grouped together, you should learn to see them all at one glance. These groups of words we will call *phrases*. Practice saying these phrases quickly at one glance:

Do you see	He has made his web	ready to pounce
the spider	and there he sits	upon a fly
in the picture	in the very middle of it	

Notice the phrases in the next story. Try to read each phrase as if it were only one word. Do not pause in the middle of it. After you have read the story through once, write a list of all the things about spiders in this story that you knew before. Make another list of the things you did not know before. Tell the story of the spider that saved his life by making a bridge.

The Spider ^(S)

Do you see the spider
in the picture?
He has just made his web,
and there he sits
in the very middle of it,
ready to pounce*
upon a fly.
The spider loves to work.
He begins to work
as soon as he begins to live.
Every spider is born a spinner.*
Even the youngest spider
knows how to spin his thread
just as well as the oldest.
The spider never has to go to school
to learn his task.
God has given him the power to do his work.
And that is why
he never makes any blunders.
He weaves his web in a most wonderful way.
Not all the weavers* and spinners
in the world could beat the spider
in the work that he does.

The spider is never in a hurry.
He takes care to make every thread fast.
He takes pride in doing his work well.
All spiders
have not the same kind of work to do.
But they all do it in the very best way.
Some spiders are masons.*
They build houses the size of a big thimble.
They make doors to them,
which they shut when they go in.
The garden spider
lets his threads float in the air
till they happen to take hold of a plant
or the branch of a tree.
He then uses these threads
as roads or bridges
by which he crosses from place to place.
A strange story is told of a spider
that saved his life by this means.
He was put upon the end of a stick
which stood a foot or two out of water.
He was on a little island* in a little sea.
What did he do?
He walked down the stick

to the edge of the water.
He went round and round it,
but he could find no way to get off.

He then went once more
to the top of the stick,
and kept still for a while.
He seemed to say to himself,
"Well, I am in a nice fix now.
What am I to do?"

He soon made up his mind.
He at once began to spin a long thread.
He made one end of it fast
to the top of the stick.
He let the thread float away in the wind,
till it caught a tree on the shore.
He then slid along this line,
and was soon safe on dry land.

Comprehension Test. See how many of these questions you can answer after reading the story the *first* time.

1. What can every spider do? Who taught him?
2. What kind of spider makes houses with doors? Did you ever see one of these houses?
3. What spider builds bridges? How does he do it? Did you ever watch a spider build a bridge?

Thought Questions

1. What is the difference between *spinning* and *weaving?*
2. What good lesson can you learn from a spider?
3. How long did it take you to read this story through and answer correctly all the questions?
4. How many words in this story have a star after them? Can you guess the meaning of each word?

Uncle Phil's Story ^(S)

Read this story and the next silently. Then decide which you like the better, and study that one until you can read or tell it well to the rest of the class. "Uncle Phil's Story" could be read orally as a dialogue. How many persons would be needed to read the parts? Read each phrase as if it were one word. How far can you read in two minutes?

"Once, when I was a little boy,"
said Uncle Phil, "I asked my mother
to let Roy and me go and play by the river.
My mother said we might go.

So we went and had a good deal of sport.
After a while, I took a shingle for a boat
and sailed it along the bank.
At last, it began to get into deep water
where I could not reach it with a stick.

"I told Roy to go and bring it to me.
Roy almost always did as I told him,
but this time he did not.
I scolded him, and he ran toward home.
Then I was very angry.
I picked up a stone and threw it at him
as hard as I could."

"Oh, Uncle Phil!" cried Archie.

"Just then, Roy turned his head,
and the stone hit him over the eyes."

"Oh, Uncle Phil!" cried Robert.

"Yes; it made him stagger.
He gave a little cry and fell to the ground.
I did not go to him,
but waded into the water for my boat.

"But it was deeper than I thought.
Before I knew it, I was in a strong current.*
I screamed as it carried me down stream,
but no one was near to help me.

"As I went down under the deep water, something took hold of me and dragged me toward the shore.

When I was safe on the bank, I saw it was Roy that had saved my life."

"Good fellow! Was he your cousin?" asked Robert.

"No," replied Uncle Phil.

"What did you say?" asked Archie.

"I put my arms around the dear fellow's neck, and begged him to forgive me."

"What did he say?" asked both the boys.

"He said, 'Bow, wow, wow!'"

"Why! Who was Roy, anyway?" they asked, in surprise.

"He was my dog," said Uncle Phil, "the best dog I ever saw. I have never been unkind to a dog or any other animal since, and I hope *you* never will be."

The Dog With a Lantern [S]

Find something in this story which proves that this dog was intelligent. Find something which proves that he was faithful; that he was persevering.

In reading, think of each phrase as one word. How far can you read in two minutes?

Here is a dog with a lantern in his mouth. His name is Carlo. He is looking for his master.

Carlo had been taught to be useful. In the place where his master lived, the roads were often so bad that, on dark nights, it was not safe for any person to go out without a light. So Carlo's master had taught him to carry a lantern for him at night. And he did it just as well as any boy could have done.

Carlo never trotted too far ahead. He kept near at hand so that the bright light of the lantern might guide his master's steps. When he came to any part of the road where there was a deep rut or hole, he would turn around to his master, as much as to say, "Take care, master! There is a hole here."

The dog's master lived about a mile from the town. When he could not get home before dark, Carlo used to be sent with the lantern to meet him.

"Come, Carlo, go for master!" was the order. And it never had to be given twice. Carlo knew where to go, quite as well as he knew the road which his master would take.

But Carlo did not always find his master at once. When he reached the town, he would run to a house, where he knew his master often was. Still holding the lantern, he would scratch at the door and bark, as much as to say, "Here I am, master, with the lantern. Are you ready for home?"

Some one would perhaps come to the door and say, "Your master is not here, Carlo." Carlo would growl, as if he meant to say, "Then he is somewhere else, and I must find him."

He would then run to one house after another, until he found his master. Then the two would start together for home.

Hero and Jet (S2)

Read this story until you find out how Hero got his name. Did he deserve the name? Why? How do you suppose Jet got *her* name?

Your teacher will time you, calling, "Mark!" at the end of two or three minutes. What is your average reading rate a minute? Mark it on your rate graph.

9 Bessie lived on a large farm in the coun-
17 try. The house was very old, and the trees
25 around it were old, too. But such apples,
31 and pears, and cherries Bessie thought
35 never grew anywhere else!
42 There were a great many chickens and
50 cows in the farmyard. Bessie used to play

with them all. They seemed to know that the little girl would not do them any harm. But her *pets* were the big dog, Hero,* and the little cat, named Jet.*

"Such apples!"

One day, when Bessie was a little girl, she was playing on the grass with her pet dog. His name was Fi′do then. While they were playing, a big, wicked-looking dog came running right up to Bessie.

Fido would not let his little mistress be hurt if he could help it. He put himself right in front of her and barked as loud as he could. As the big dog tried to go past him, he caught him by the tail and held on tight. The bad dog got many a bump and some pretty hard bites.

Soon Bessie's mamma came and drove the naughty dog away. Then they all petted Fido, and papa changed his name to Hero because he had been so brave. Ever since that time, Bessie loved him more than ever.

One day, Hero found a little black kitten away down the road somewhere, and brought it home. He laid it in Bessie's lap. Then he looked into her face as much as to say, "Please take care of him for my sake." Bessie named the little black kitten, Jet. From that time, Hero and Jet were always together.

Bessie never forgot how Hero had taken care of her. She never forgot that he liked his breakfast and supper of nice new milk. Every morning and every evening, when the maids were going out to milk the cows, you might have seen Bessie walking behind them with Hero on one side, and Jet on the other. In one hand Bessie carried a little pail, and in the other a milking stool. Old Boss, the gentlest cow, knew that this little milkmaid was coming to her. She would stand very still, not even kicking the flies away, for fear of hurting the little milkmaid. Two little hands would be at work and soon the tiny pail would be full of foaming, creamy milk. Then Bessie would pour it into a deep dish for Hero and Jet to drink.

Oral Reading

Once more, boys and girls, you are to have a talk with your teacher about *learning to read*. You have now had a number of lessons on *silent* reading. What fun it has been, hasn't it, to see how quickly you could find out what the story was about?

Silent reading is very important, but if all your reading were silent, much of the good you might do for others would be lost. If you learn to read well out loud, you can often give real pleasure to others, and help them, too. Do you know any blind person or some aged man or woman, or some one who is sick, who lives near by? It would bring great joy to them for you to take your reader and visit them some day. How thankful they would be to hear you read a good story in an interesting way! In their prayers, I am sure they would say, "God bless that noble boy or girl."

Your father or mother or your little brother or sister would like to hear you read, too, I am sure. And you would want to do your very best for them. When you can read well enough, you might be needed to read a story to the whole school or perhaps even to a parents' meeting. So get ready, boys and girls, and your chance will come.

How can you get ready? That is just what I am going to tell you. There are four things to work for in *oral* reading, for that is what reading out loud is called.

First. You must not only *understand* what you are reading, but you must try to sympathize with the people you are reading about. If it is a sad story, you should feel sorry. If it is a happy story, you should feel glad. Try to read the words spoken in the same tone that you think the people spoke them. Sometimes it will be slow and thoughtful. Sometimes it will be with surprise. Try to find out just how the different ones in the story *felt*, and then read what they said in the same tone that *they* spoke.

Second. In learning to read orally, you must be sure to pro-nounce′ your words correctly and very dis-tinct′ly. If you mumble your words or run them together, others cannot understand you, and they will not enjoy listening to you. Practice much on this part of your reading.

Third. Read only the words that are in the story. Be careful not to leave out some or put in others, as this might change the meaning. Be careful, too, not to read in a stumbling way, or go back and repeat words you have already read. Read slowly enough so that your reading will be smooth and even. If you read too hurriedly, the people who listen will find it hard to get all the thought, and they will soon become tired of listening to you.

Fourth. The fourth thing to remember in oral reading is to read *to* the one who is listening. Read as you would *talk*. When you talk to some one, you don't look down at your nose all the time, do you? Oh no! You look right into the eyes of the one to whom you speak. That is the way to read. Have your story so well prepared that you almost know parts of it by heart. Then often look away from your story and straight into the eyes of those who are listening. If you know your story well enough, you will not lose your place when you need to look again at your reader.

The next story is named "The Echo." It is a fine one for oral reading. Have you ever heard an echo? You surely have if you have ever lived among the hills. Your voice goes out and seems to strike the side of a hill. Then it bounds back somewhat as a ball bounds back when you throw it against a building. The echo says exactly what *you* said. Only the voice seems far away.

As you read "The Echo" orally, try to give the words of the echo a real echo sound. Find out what lesson the echo taught Henry. Part of this story could be read as a dialogue. How many persons would be needed to read it that way?

Try to read each line as one phrase. This will help you to read more smoothly.

The Echo ^(o)

"Hop, hop, hop!" shouted little Henry, who was playing one day in a field near a wood.

"Hop, hop, hop!" came an echo* back to him.

"Who is there?" asked Henry in surprise.

"Who is there?" answered the echo.

"Foolish fellow!" cried Henry at the top of his voice.

"Foolish fellow!" came from the wood.

At this, Henry became very angry,

and called out many ugly names.
The voice from the wood
sent back every word.

Henry could not see
who was speaking from the wood.
He ran home to his father
as fast as he could.

"Father, a boy who is hid in the woods
has been calling me bad names," he said.

"Ah, Henry," said his father,
"you have heard nothing
but the echo of your own words.
The bad names came first
from your own lips.
Had you used kind and gentle words,
you would have had
kind and gentle words in return.
Kind words bring back kind echoes."

Robert Louis Stevenson [S]

This story is about a little sick boy who was always cheerful and kind. As you read it, find out this little boy's name, where he lived, and what he planned to be when he became a man. When must it have been hard for him to be kind? How far can you read silently in three minutes?

1. When Robert Louis Stevenson was a little boy, he always went to bed at seven o'clock. In the winter time, this seemed all right to him, for then it was dark at that hour. But in the summer time it was broad daylight at seven o'clock and for a long time after that. Then it was not so easy to have to go to bed while the birds were still hopping about, and he did *so* want to play a little longer. He couldn't understand about the days getting longer in summer.

"I'd rather go to bed at the seven o'clock that *used* to be," he would say to his mother.

But Robert Louis was a sickly child, and his wise mother knew that the best thing for him was plenty of sleep and rest.

2. When he was grown up, he wrote a great many poems especially for children. One of them he named "Bed in Summer." He thought other little boys and girls who like to play late in the summer evenings instead of going to bed at their reg'u-lar time would enjoy reading it.

3. Sometimes, little Robert Louis was too

sick to sleep, and he would lie awake all night long. He would cough until his poor little body seemed all tired out. But he had a very kind nurse. When he could not sleep, she would often read to him stories from the Bible. Sometimes she would gently take him up in her arms and carry him to the window where he could look out at the stars. If they saw lights in other houses, they wondered if there were other sick little boys there with their nurses, waiting for the morning. How glad Robert Louis was when he could hear horses and people begin to pass by on the street in the early morning! Even when he became a grown-up man, he never forgot this kind, faithful nurse.

"It seems to me that I should have died," he said, "if I had been left there alone to cough and weary in the darkness. My patient nurse was like an angel to help and comfort me."

4. All through his boyhood he planned to be an author.* One day, before he was old enough to write, he began to print a

story of Moses. It was such a long story that his mother helped him at last by writing down what he told her.

5. When he became a man, he wrote a book called "A Child's Garden of Verse." In this book there are a number of very pretty poems that children love. He wrote most of these poems in a dark room because his eyes were so bad that they could not bear the light. He wrote them with his left hand because his right hand was injured and had to be carried in a sling. He could not tell some one else what to write for him because when he talked, it would set him to coughing, and then blood would come from his lungs. So the doctor said he must not speak.

Robert Louis Stevenson

6. All this time Robert Louis Stevenson's

home was in Scotland. He loved his country, but the climate was too cold for him. When he became a man, he took his family and went to Sa-mo'a, an island* in the warm waters of the South Pacific Ocean. Here Mr. Stevenson began to grow stronger. He felt so much better in this warm climate that he decided to build a home in Samoa.

7. He bought four hundred acres of land covered with trop'i-cal* trees and bushes and vines. It was a real jungle,* and Mrs. Stevenson could not get through it until a trail* was cut through the wild forest. The trail went up a hill, and at the top, they built their house. Here and there along the trail grew coconut palms and other trees that do not grow in colder climates.

8. In his Samoan home Mr. Stevenson grew quite well and strong. He worked hard clearing the land for a little garden. He often went boating and bathing.

9. The native Samoans loved Mr. Stevenson. He used to amuse them by telling them stories. Because of this, they called

him "Tu-si-ta′la" instead of Mr. Stevenson. Tusitala is a Samoan word which means "Teller of Tales."

10. But Tusitala did more than amuse the natives. He helped them. When they were sick, he cared for them. When they were hungry, he gave them food. When they were in trouble, he told them what to do. He never thought about their skin being brown instead of white. He just treated them as brothers.

And these un-civ′il-ized natives returned his kindness. Long lines of them often came to his home with baskets filled with presents. Some of the Samoan chiefs made a fine new road to his house. They did all the work and paid all the cost themselves. Then they named it "The Road of the Loving Heart."

11. Where "The Road of the Loving Heart" meets the main road, Tusitala placed a signboard. The writing on it is in the native language, and means, "It shall never be muddy; it shall go on forever;

this road that we have dug." This signboard is still there, and if you ever go to Samoa you can see it, and walk over the road.

When the road was finished, Mr. Stevenson gave a feast to all the natives. The tablecloth, made of green banana leaves, was spread on the ground, and the people sat around it on mats. Banana leaves were used for plates.

12. Mr. and Mrs. Stevenson sometimes visited other islands. Wherever they went, they made friends. Once, they went to an island whose king was a savage fellow. This king would not let a white man land on his island. But he liked the looks of Mr. Stevenson, and received him as a guest. Mr. and Mrs. Stevenson stayed on the island for some time. When they left, this savage king wept.

"You no see king cry before," he said through his tears. "King all the same man, feel bad, he cry. I very sorry! I very sorry!"

13. When Mr. Stevenson died, every one on the island mourned. The great flag was

taken down from the housetop and wrapped around his body. The brown chiefs quietly and lovingly covered him with fine mats. They would not go away from his side. They wanted to spend the last night with him.

Loving hands cleared a road up the mountain to the place which he had chosen for his grave. Samoan friends carried his casket* up the steep path. The others followed on foot.

By the side of the grave of their beloved Tusitala, the natives planted a Scotch thistle. The thistle is the national* flower of Scotland, his native country. On his tomb is written a verse from the Samoan Bible.

Since his death, the Samoan chiefs have not allowed anyone to use guns on the hillside where he lies. They want the birds to sing there without fear.

14. In spite of all his sickness and his short life, Robert Louis Stevenson did a great work. But the greatest thing he did was to be so unselfish and kind to all that he filled their hearts with love and cheer.

—*Adapted.*

Comprehension Test. How many of these questions can you answer correctly after reading the story the *first* time?
1. Why do you think Robert Louis didn't like to go to bed?
2. Who was his first story about?
3. What book did he write for children?
   How did he have to do it?
4. In what country was he born?
   Find it on the globe.
5. Why did he go to Samoa to live?
   Find Samoa on the globe.
6. What did the natives on the island call him?
7. What did they build for him?
   What did they name it?
8. Tell a story showing that the people loved him.
9. What is the greatest work he did?
10. What is the national flower of Scotland?
    What is the national flower of your country?

Bed in Summer [87]

Who wrote this poem?

When Robert Louis Stevenson was a little boy, he could not understand why he had to get up at night in the winter, and go to bed by day in the summer. Can you explain this?

Notice the tone your teacher uses as she reads this poem to you. Then as you read, try to use the same tone.

1. In winter, I get up at night,
   And dress by yellow candlelight.
   In summer, quite the other way,
   I have to go to bed by day.

2. I have to go to bed and see
   The birds still hopping in the tree,
   Or hear the grown-up people's feet
   Still going past me in the street.

3. And does it not seem hard to you,
   When all the sky is clear and blue,
   And I should like *so much* to play,
   To have to *go to bed* by *day?*

   —*Robert Louis Stevenson.*

Memory Reading

Boys and girls, to-day you are to have another talk with your teacher about learning to read. In your past lessons you have learned something about *silent* reading. You have also been learning about *oral* reading. There is still another way to read, and this you do without looking at your book.

You don't see how you can do that? I will tell you. You can memorize some of the poems that you like, and then read these beautiful poems to others without looking at your reader.

By learning to read well from memory, you can give much pleasure to others, for every one likes to hear a good poem well recited. In your third reader there are many beautiful little poems for you to enjoy. In some of these there are such beautiful word pictures or such happy thoughts that you will want to remember them as long as you live. Think carefully about all the poems in your reader, and choose for memory those you like best.

Some children think it is hard to memorize poetry. But that is not true. It seems hard to them only because they have never learned how to do it. This year you are going to learn how to memorize poems easily and quickly.

Suppose you try memorizing the poem you have just had in class,—the one written by Robert Louis Stevenson, named "Bed in Summer." You have learned how little Robert Louis had to go to bed even before the birds were quiet. And you know how hard it was for him to stop playing and do this, just as it would be hard for you. You have heard your teacher read this poem to you, and now you can read it just as well as she did!

Try reading the first stanza with your teacher. Then, read it alone, and see how much you can look away from your book while still reading. How many times do you have to read it before you can read it without looking at your book at all?

Read the second stanza silently. As you read, try to see the birds hopping in the tree, and hear the tramping of people in the street. How many of you after two minutes' study can read this stanza without looking at the book?

Try the third stanza in the same way. You are now ready to recite the whole poem. How easy it was, wasn't it? And I imagine most of you learned it all in not more than five minutes.

It is really very easy to learn to repeat a few stanzas of poetry, and it takes only a very little time after you once get to work. But it isn't quite so easy to remember it until to-morrow or next week or next year. And the poems you learn in school you should be able to recite at any time during the year.

The best way to do this is to review them often. Say them over to yourself after you have learned your other lessons. Say them to one another at recess or sometime outside of school hours. Say them at home to your little brothers or sisters or to your parents. And when you can say them well, you may be asked to recite them when some one comes to visit the school. Always be ready. And do your part well.

Do you see the number 58 after the name of the next poem? It means that there are 58 words in the poem. After each of the best poems in your reader there is a number which tells how many words are in it. How many words in "A Mother's Song" on page 38. How many in "Bed in Summer"?

These numbers are given so that you may keep track of how much memory work you do each school period, and so that your teacher will know what grade to give you in memory reading at the close of the period. In order to get a passing grade of 75, you should learn a poem or poems that contain at least 120 words. If you learn 140 words, you will be given a grade of 80; 160 words gives you a grade of 85; 200 words a grade of 90; 250 words a grade of 95; 300 words a grade of 100. I wonder how many of you are going to get a grade of 100 each period of this school year. *Do it*, boys and girls!

Bedtime ⁽⁵⁸⁾

There is a pretty word picture in the first stanza of "Bedtime." Tell what it looks like to you. What are the "curtains of purple and red"?

The birdie has gone to its nest,
   And baby must go to her bed,
For the sun has sunk down in the west
   In curtains of purple and red.

Yes, this is the end of the day;
   The lambs are asleep in the dew;
So baby must leave off her play,
   And go to *her* little bed, too.
                  —*Author Unknown.*

A Mother's Song [65]

This little poem tells us how the songs we learn in childhood help us when we are grown up. What song does your mother sing that you like best? What song do you know of "the beautiful home above"?

A mother sang to her child one day
   A song of the beautiful home above;
Sang it as only a woman sings
   Whose heart is full of a mother's love.

And many a time in the years that came
   He heard the sound of that low,
      sweet song:
It took him back to his childhood days;
   It kept his feet from the paths of wrong.

—*Author Unknown.*

Which poem do you like the better—"Bedtime" or "A Mother's Song"? Which three pupils in the class can be the first to read from memory the poem of your choice?

Little "John Peter" (S)

As you read this story silently, see how many things John Peter did which show that he was a real little Christian. There is a beautiful promise in Matthew 5:10 for such children as he. Read it, and tell what this promise is.

Your teacher will time you as you read, and at the end of each minute, you may mark the place where you are reading. How long does it take you to read the story through?

This is a good story to practice reading out loud, so that you can read it to some one who has never heard it.

---

1. This is a story about a little boy who lives in Rou-ma′ni-a. Roumania is a country in Eu′rope.

I do not know this boy's name. It might have been Peter, for he stood like a rock for the right. It might have been John, for his heart was full of love. Let us call him John Peter.

2. John Peter is nine years of age. He loves to go to Sabbath school. But the law of Roumania says that all children must go to public school on Saturday as well as on other days.

If they are absent from school, their parents must pay a fine. They must pay sixty-five lei.* It takes about two lei to make one cent. Sixty-five lei is about thirty cents. That is a good deal of money in Roumania at this time. It means much more than thirty cents means in America.

3. But John Peter loved the Sabbath school. He loved to sing the beautiful songs about Jesus. He loved his kind Sabbath school teacher. He loved to listen to the Bible stories. He wanted to go to Sabbath school every Sabbath. He did not want to miss a single lesson.

"Mother," he said, "the lessons I learn in Sabbath school are worth more than sixty-five lei."

John Peter's mother loved her darling boy. She was very happy because he loved the Sabbath school where he was taught the word of God.

"You may go to Sabbath school, my boy," she said, "and I will pay the fine."

So John Peter went to Sabbath school,

and his mother paid the fine. Again and again the lad was absent from school. Again and again his mother paid the fine.

It was hard for her to save so much money every week. But she wanted her little boy to learn God's word. She wanted him to love the Sabbath always. She was glad to work hard and save the money.

4. The teacher wondered why John Peter was absent so often.

"Why are you absent from school on Saturday?" she asked at last.

"I go to Sabbath school on Sabbath," John Peter said politely.

The teacher thought that was a poor reason for being absent from school. She did not love the Sabbath. What did she care for the Sabbath school? She was vexed.

"I shall punish you if you are absent again," she said.

5. Poor little boy! What should he do? Every day he thought about it. At last, another Sabbath came.

"Shall I go to Sabbath school where God wants me?" he asked himself. "Or shall I go to school where the teacher wants me?" He decided to obey God, no matter what came.

6. When he went to school on Monday, he paid his fine as usual. But now he must be punished also. The teacher made fun of his religion. She thought if John Peter wanted to be so religious, she would give him a chance *every* day.

"You may kneel in the corner of the room for four hours every day of this week," she said sternly.

All the children were watching little John Peter. It was hard for him to have his religion made fun of in that way. But he walked quietly over to the corner of the room. He knelt down on the floor. No doubt all the children laughed at him. Poor little John Peter!

7. Five minutes passed, then ten minutes, then fifteen. How long it seemed! Half an hour passed at last. He was getting very

tired. But he knew that he had done nothing wrong.

Slowly the clock on the wall ticked away one hour. How his poor little body ached! But he did not complain. He knew Jesus had suffered more than that for him. At last the weary day drew to a close.

The next day it was just the same—kneeling four long hours in the corner. Then Wednesday came, and with it another four hours in the corner. Thursday came, and at its close, the tired little boy went home.

"Only one more day now before the happy Sabbath!" he thought. How glad he would be to see his loving Sabbath school teacher!

8. On Friday, little John Peter knelt in the corner as usual. It was the prep-a-ra′-tion* day for the Sabbath. Did he remember how Jesus knelt on the damp earth for hours? Did he remember that Jesus prayed, "Father, forgive them"? *Did* he remember, I wonder?

Do you think his long punishment made him feel like giving up the Sabbath school? Oh no! He longed more than ever to see his Sabbath school teacher. She loved him, he knew.

9. At last his week of punishment was over. The time till Sabbath school should begin seemed almost as long as the hours of his punishment. But at last it came, and little John Peter skipped happily away to Sabbath school.

He told his teacher all about it. How proud she felt of her brave, loyal little boy! She put her arms lovingly around him.

"What did you think about all the time you were kneeling?" she asked gently.

And what do you suppose he told her? Was he thinking how cross and cruel his teacher was? Was he thinking that when he had a good chance he would cause her trouble? What *was* he thinking about, I wonder?

"I prayed that the Lord would forgive my teacher," he softly whispered.

The Tree Frog ^(S3)

This story is your third special rate drill for this period. Find your silent reading rate, and mark it on the graph in the back of your reader. As you read, find out the difference between a tree frog and a bullfrog.

A tree frog is only about one and a half inches long.

1. The tree frog does not live in the pond with the bullfrogs. His home is in a tree. Sometimes he looks out of a knot hole. Sometimes he clings close to the tree trunk. Often he swings happily from the under side of a leaf.

He is so nearly the color of the tree that it is hard to see him even when he is in plain sight. Once a man marked a tree frog, and learned that for four years he kept the same home in an old hickory tree.

2. When the tree frog is hungry, he sits very still and darts out his sticky tongue at insects that fly past him.

He is so pleased when rain is near that he sings a little song. It is, "R-r-r-d! R-r-r-d!" Have you ever heard him sing?

The tree frog is a climber. The knobs or pads on the ends of his toes help him to climb.

3. When winter comes, he climbs down from his tree and burrows* in the leaf mold.* Sometimes he makes his bed in a hollow tree.

His big cousins, the bullfrogs, wrap themselves in mud blankets and sleep at the bottom of the pond. When spring comes, all the frogs awake, and sing and sing for joy.

A Bullfrog

4. A lady once saw a tree frog as he was peeping out of his knot hole. She lifted him carefully and took him into her house. She went to a window where plants were growing.

The tree frog was much frightened. He sat very still in her hand with his legs folded close to his body.

When the lady opened her hand, he saw the green leaves. He thought, "Here is my chance to get away." So he made a flying leap. But he did not get away. He landed among the plants.

Then he saw a tree close by. He made another leap, hoping to reach it. Something hard and slippery kept him from the tree. He could not see this thing, but he found that he could climb up.

The little children watched him climb. Their mother showed them his webbed feet and long, slender toes. They saw that each one was tipped with a little knob.

To show them how he could change color, she placed him on something black. Soon his skin grew quite dark.

Then she placed him on something green. After he had been on the green for a time, his color grew greenish.

After the children had asked all the questions they could think of, they all went out to the tree, and the lady put him in his knot hole.

I think he was glad to be at home again, don't you?

—*Gordon Third Reader.*

Comprehension Test. Answer as many of these questions as you can after you have read the story *only once*. If you fail on any question, study the story until you find all the answers.

1. Where is the home of a tree frog?
2. Where is the home of a bullfrog?
3. Where does the bullfrog stay in winter?
4. Where does the tree frog stay in winter?
5. What is the color of a tree frog?
6. How does a tree frog eat? What does he eat?
7. How does a tree frog climb?
8. Tell the story about the tree frog that a lady caught.
9. Did you ever see a tree frog? Is it as large as a bullfrog?

The Sun's Travels [77]

Who wrote this poem? What other poems of his do you know?

Read stanza one carefully. Read the line that tells where the sun goes at night.

In stanza two read the lines that tell what the children in India are doing when the children on the other side of the globe are playing. Ask your teacher to explain this. On the globe find India, Scotland, the Atlantic Sea, and "the West."

Read the lines that tell what the children in the West are doing when those in the East (in Scotland where Robert Louis lived when he was a boy) are just finishing their supper. Can you explain this?

1. The sun is not abed when I
   At night upon my pillow lie;
   Still round the earth his way he takes,
   And morning after morning makes.

2. While here at home, in shining day,
   We round the sunny garden play,
   Each little Indian sleepyhead
   Is being kissed and put to bed.

3. And when at eve I rise from tea,
   Day dawns beyond the Atlantic Sea,
   And all the children in the West
   Are getting up and being dressed.
   —*Robert Louis Stevenson.*

The Cloud [88]

It will be interesting for one child to be the cloud, and read what the cloud says, and the other pupils ask the questions of the cloud. Remember that good oral reading is slow enough to be distinct.

What three things do these stanzas tell that the clouds do?

What are you doing, little white cloud,
Up in the heavens, sailing so proud?
Helping my brothers here in the blue
Hide the hot sunshine, children, from you.

Where are you going, flying so slow,
White cloud so lazy, I'd like to know?
Gathering raindrops out of the air,
For the poor flowers, dying down there.

When will you scatter some of the showers
You have been saving, down to the flowers?
Where the Lord sends me, always I roam,
When the Lord bids me, children, I'll come.

—*Author Unknown.*

Babyland [97]

Find five questions in this poem, and tell the answer to each. Suppose one pupil reads the questions, calling upon others in the class to read the answers.

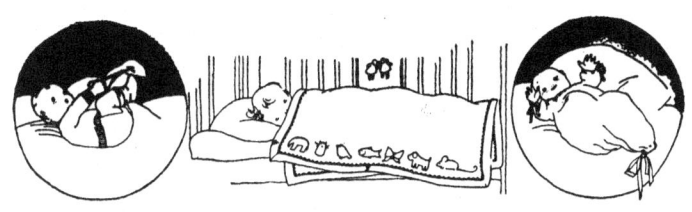

1. "How many miles to Babyland?"--
    "Anyone can tell;
        Up one flight,
        To your right;
    Please to ring the bell."

2. "What can you *see* in Babyland?"—
    "Little folks in white,
        Downy* heads,
        Cradle beds,
    Faces pure and bright!"

3. "What do they *do* in Babyland?"—
    "Dream, and wake, and play,
        Laugh and crow,
        Shout and grow;
    Jolly times have they!"

4. "What do they *say* in Babyland?"—
    "Why, the *oddest things!*
        Might as well
        Try to tell
    What a birdie sings!"

5. "Who is the *queen* of Babyland?"—
   "Mother, kind and sweet;
   And her love,
   Born above,
   Guides the little feet."

   —*George Cooper.*

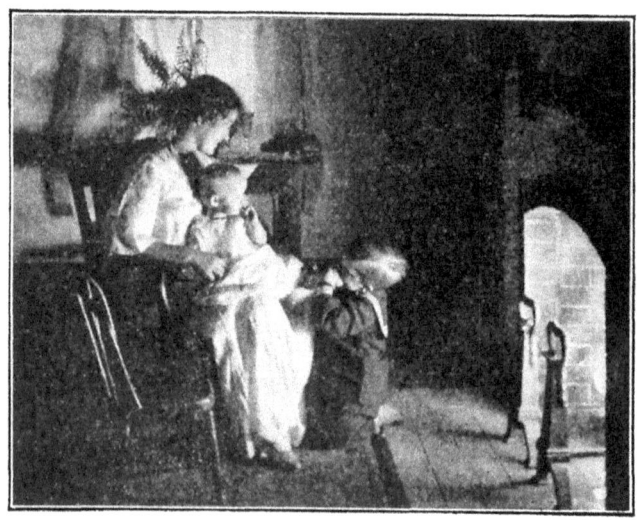

"The Queen of Babyland"

The Mt. Roraima Church School ^(s)

This story is about a church school of Indians away down in South America. Find South America on the globe. Find Mt. Ro-rai′ma* on the map of South America.

Read and find out how this church school is different from yours. Read Isaiah 40:31, and tell which of the children in this school you think will love this promise the most.

How far can you read silently in three minutes?

---

1. The Mt. Roraima church school is in South America. It was started in 1928. Thirty-four children attend this school. They are all Indians. Mrs. Elizabeth Cott is their teacher. This story is from what she has written about them.

2. These little Indian children are very anxious to learn. They love to learn Bible memory verses. They love to sing songs about Jesus. They sing some of the same songs that you sing. These songs help them to do right.

3. When the children first came to this church school, they were very dirty. No one had ever taught them that they should come to school with clean hands and faces. The teacher taught them to sing:

"I washed my hands this morning,
O very clean and white,
And lent them both to Jesus,
To work for Him till night."

Now, as soon as they hear the call for school, they scramble down the hill to the waterfall close by. They nearly fall over one another to see who will reach the water first. In a moment, off comes their one-piece dress, and into the water they plunge for a good bath. They have no towels to dry themselves, but the hot sun soon dries them. Then they dress and come straight to school.

4. One day, a little boy named Daniel came to school with dirty hands and face. In a few minutes all the children were singing, "I washed my hands this morning."

Daniel looked down at his dirty hands. He could not sing the song, for he had not washed his hands. You should have seen how guilty he looked. He knew he could not work for Jesus with dirty hands. He left the room quickly. Down to the waterfall he ran as fast as his feet could carry him. Before the other children had stopped singing, he was back in school. His hands and face were nice and clean, but dripping with water. I don't think he forgot again, do you?

5. During prayer, the children all kneel with both knees on the ground. Every eye is closed. Sometimes they hold them tightly with their fingers, so that they cannot come

These are the Mt. Roraima church school children wearing the new dresses Mrs. Cott made for them. How would you like to visit their school? Can you find little Marguerite?

open. Some bow with their faces to the ground. They are very quiet during prayer.

6. These little children can sing "The Boat on Galilee," "Jesus Knows All About Our Troubles," "Jesus Is Coming Again," and several other beautiful hymns. Little Marguerite, the baby of the school, can sing all by herself, "Jesus Loves Me, This I

Know." These children can say "The Lord's Prayer" and a number of Bible verses. They are also learning to read and write. They love to write on the slates that have been sent to them.

7. One little girl's name is Ella. She is a little cripple.* She cannot go to school. She lives in one of the huts at the mission. She has no parents to care for her. She says that when Jesus comes, she is going to live with Him, and she will have two wings and fly like a bird. Shall we not pray for these little Indian children, that they may be ready to meet Jesus when He comes?

Comprehension Test

1. In what country is the Mt. Roraima church school?
2. What kind of children attend this school?
3. How long ago was this school started?
4. What do the children love to learn?
5. Name one song that they love to sing.
6. How do they get ready for school?
7. What little boy once forgot to get ready?
8. How do they behave during prayer?
9. What song can Baby Marguerite sing all alone?
10. What is the name of the little cripple girl?

Taught by a Parrot [O]

Johnny is a rather careless boy. He often forgets the good manners his mother tries to teach him. One day, she sent him to Mrs. Grey's on an errand. When the lady came to the door, he told his errand without taking off his hat. Suddenly, a hoarse voice croaked out, "Take off your hat! Take off your hat!"

Astonished and half frightened, Johnny snatched it off.

At this, Mrs. Grey laughed.

"It is only my parrot," she said. "Polly likes to remind everybody of his duty, you see."

"Yes, Mrs. Grey," said Johnny. But he thought to himself that it was a great pity if he had to be taught manners by a parrot. He made up his mind to be more careful in the future.

—*Selected.*

A Spelling Stairway ^(S)

Read this story silently and mark your reading rate. Then tell how a spelling lesson is like a stairway. How many holes did *you* leave in *your* spelling stairway to-day?

The conversation between Jimmy and the carpenter would make a good dialogue for oral reading. Try it, reading only the words spoken by each one.

₇ Jimmy came in from school and began
₁₃ to climb into his play clothes.
₁₉ "How was your spelling to-day?" grand-
₂₁ father asked.
₂₇ "Missed only one little word," answered
₃₅ Jimmy. Then he ran out whistling, and over
₄₃ to the new house next door. Every night
₅₁ since the new house had been started, Jimmy
₅₇ had watched the carpenter after school.
₆₄ "How hard did you study to-day?" called
₆₆ the carpenter.
₇₅ "Oh, I only missed one word out of ten,"
₇₇ said Jimmy.
₈₃ The carpenter stopped pounding for a
₉₁ moment and looked down at Jimmy as if
₉₈ he were interested in those ten words
₁₀₂ Jimmy was telling about.

"Now isn't that queer!" he said.

"What?" asked Jimmy in surprise.

"Why, your work to-day was something like mine."

"I don't see what you mean," said Jimmy.

"You had to learn ten words in your spelling lesson, and I had to build ten steps in this stairway," the carpenter answered, with a twinkle in his eye. Then he picked up his hammer to go to work again.

"You didn't miss any step in your stairway, though, did you?" the boy said rather softly as if he were just a little ashamed.

"Well, no. They're all in good and tight. I couldn't keep my job very long if I should miss one step in ten," laughed the jolly carpenter.

The next day, when Jimmy came in from school, grandfather asked him the very same question:

"How was spelling to-day, my boy?"

"Well, I'm going to tell the carpenter to-night that no one will tumble through my spelling stairway, for I didn't leave any holes," he said.

Signboards to Healthland [S]

 is for Tub where a bath we will seek.
If we're wise, it will be more than once in each week.

 is for Out and for Open-air play.
Out of doors we must work for a while every day.

 is for Health in the water we drink.
Drink six glasses a day, and 'twill keep the face pink.

 is for Eating the food that we should—
Every day some fresh fruit and some vegetables good.

 is for Air that we breathe every night,
With our windows wide open from dark until light.

 is for Light in the eyes, clear and bright,
Never read by a dim light, either daytime or night.

 is for Teeth. They'll be healthy and white
If they're brushed after meals, or at least morn and night.

 is for Happy. We'll feel fine as silk
If we leave tea and coffee, and drink good sweet milk."

Comprehension Test
1. This rime spells a "health acrostic." What is an acrostic?* What does this acrostic spell?
2. Which signboard points to "Daily Exercise"?
3. Which one points to "Care for Your Teeth"?
4. Which one points to "Eat Good Food"?
5. Which points to "Care for Your Eyes"?
6. Which points to "Drink Plenty of Water"?
7. Which points to "Breathe Fresh Air"?
8. Which points to "Drink No Tea or Coffee"?
9. Which points to "Drink Good Milk"?
10. Are you "detouring"* around any of them?

Tiny's Alarm Clock (O)

When did Tiny's alarm clock go off? How? What are the alarm clocks in our hearts? When did *your* alarm clock go off last? Who is it that tries to put us to sleep after our alarm clock sounds?

How many people would be needed to read this story as a dialogue? In reading, try to use the same tones of voice that you think the people in the story used. Read plainly.

Tiny looked up from her slate as her big brother, Kent, came in one day with an odd-shaped paper bundle in his hands. Tiny ran to meet him.

"Oh, Kent, what is it?" she asked. "Anything for me?"

"No," said Kent. "Such a wide-awake puss as you are doesn't need an aid to early rising." And he untied the string and opened the package.

"Why, it's a clock!" said Tiny, disappointed. "We have *three* clocks now, Kent. What made you buy another?"

"You just listen," said Kent, as he began winding the little clock. "It's an alarm clock," he explained, smiling at Tiny's wonder. "We can set it so that the alarm will strike at any time of night, and wake us. You know I have to leave home before daylight sometimes," for Kent was an engine driver.

"How very, very funny!" said Tiny, with sparkling eyes. "Goes off all itself, without anyone's touching it! Oh, how I wish I had one!"

"There's nothing funny about it," said Kent. "If people don't mind the alarm when it strikes, but think they will sleep a little longer, they grow less likely to be waked by it, and soon it does not wake them at all."

"I wish I could have one all my own," Tiny said again. "It must be such fun to hear it go off."

"You *do* have one," said Kent soberly.

"I? An alarm clock?"

Kent nodded.

"Where?"

"Right in there," said Kent, placing his hands over Tiny's heart.

"Well, I don't believe it ever went off," laughed Tiny.

"Yes, I'm sure it has. Wait till you feel like doing something wrong. That little clock will say, 'Why, Tiny, *don't!*' You see if it doesn't."

Tiny laughed and went back to her book. Soon a call came from the kitchen.

"Tiny, dear, I want you!"

Tiny's mouth began to pout. But suddenly she thought about the alarm clock in her heart.

"Yes, mother," she called out cheerily. As she danced out of the room, she looked back to say, "It went off loud then, Kent."

Kent nodded and smiled.

"I thought it would," he said.

Boys and girls, be sure to answer the first call of your alarm clocks, or they will ring and ring in vain, and the first thing you know you will turn out good-for-nothing men and women. —*Richmond Christian Advocate.*

Little Papoose Lullaby (78)

A papoose is an Indian baby. Man'i-tou is the Indian's name for the Creator. Listen as your teacher reads this lullaby to you.

Rock-a-by, hush-a-by, little papoose,
  The stars come into the sky,
The whippoorwill's crying,
    the daylight is dying,
  The river runs murmuring by.

This is a "rock-a-by baby in the tree top," isn't it?

The pine trees are slumbering,
> little papoose,
The squirrel has gone to his nest,
The robins are sleeping,
> the mother bird's keeping
The little ones warm with her breast.

Then hush-a-by, rock-a-by, little papoose,
> You sail on the river of dreams;
Dear Manitou loves you
> and watches above you
Till time when the morning light gleams.

—*Charles Myall.*

Appreciation Study

Read the second stanza and find the picture in it. Did you ever hear a whippoorwill? What time of day does it cry? What three words in this stanza *sound* like a lullaby? Make them sound that way as you read or recite this stanza.

Read the second stanza and find the picture in it.

What picture do you see in the third stanza? Did *you* ever sail on "the river of dreams"?

Which stanza tells about the early evening when the darkness is just beginning? Which tells about a later hour when everything has gone to bed? Which tells about the long night? How do you know?

Read the whole poem aloud. Read slowly and soothingly, as if you were trying to hush a baby to sleep. Can you memorize one stanza in two minutes?

Columbus and a New World (S)

No one knows the day of Columbus' birth, so "Columbus' Day" is October 12. Read this story and find out why. After you have read it through just for the enjoyment it gives you, read it again and find on the globe the places named. Trace on the globe or map the voyage of Columbus.

Practice reading paragraphs 10 and 11 orally. Read the last part of paragraph 10 in a sad, discouraged tone. Read the first five sentences in paragraph 11 in an excited tone. Read the next two rapidly. Read the rest of the paragraph slowly. Try to feel as these men felt.

Christopher Columbus

1. Every one knows that Christopher Columbus was the man who discovered America. When Christopher was a boy, he lived in a little town in Italy, called Genoa. This town is by the sea. Christopher loved to watch the ships and talk with the sailors.

When he was fourteen years old, Christopher became a sailor himself. Then he learned all about ships. He learned about India and other countries. He heard that these countries were rich in gold and spices.

2. In those days people thought that all there was to this world was Europe, and a little of Africa and Asia. They never dreamed that Africa and Asia were *ever so much larger* than Europe. They never dreamed that across the ocean were two large countries which we now call North America and South America.

They were afraid to sail out of sight of land, for they thought some terrible serpent or some big sea animal would swallow them and their ships. They thought the earth was flat, and if they went too far, they might fall off over the edge. And then,— what would become of them?

3. Columbus was not satisfied with these ideas. He did not believe the sea was full of terrible serpents. He kept wondering what was *beyond* the great ocean. At last, he decided to sail across it and find out. He believed the earth was round like a ball. He

thought by sailing west for a few days he would go around this ball and reach India, which was east of where he lived. Travelers had often wished they could go to India in ships instead of having to go across the hot deserts on camels. Columbus believed he could find a way by water.

4. Every one laughed at his idea that the earth was round. They thought he was crazy. How could people on the other side of a round earth live with their heads down? Besides, if a ship ever got over on the other side, how could it climb back?

5. When the people in Italy would not listen to him, he went to Spain to talk with King Ferdinand and Queen Isabella. He said if they would give him ships and sailors, he would sail around the world to India, and bring back great riches to them.

King Ferdinand thought it would cost too much money to build ships that might be lost in the sea. But Isabella believed Columbus was right. She wanted him to go.

"I will give all my jewels, if necessary," she said, "to raise the money."

6. So three ships were made ready. They were named the "Santa Ma-ri′a,"* the "Pin′ta,"* and the "Niña."* On the third day of August, 1492, Columbus and about one hundred sailors started on their unknown voyage. People on shore wept, for they thought they should never see their sailor friends again.

7. After a few days, they had sailed out of sight of land. Then the sailors became frightened, and wanted to go back home. But Columbus was not afraid. Their ships did not fall off the edge of the earth. They saw no sea serpents. The sky was blue and the wind kept them sailing westward.

8. A week passed, but they saw no land. Another week, and still no land. Another week, and nothing but water all around them.

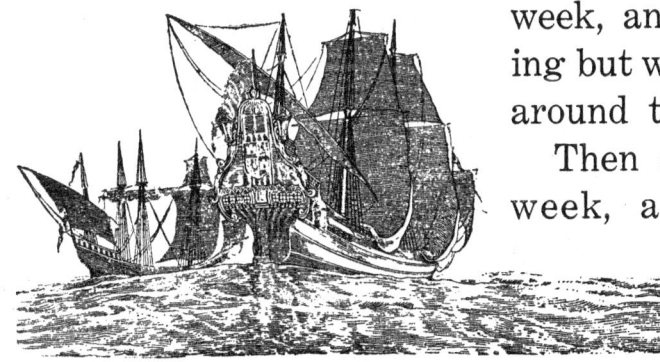

Then another week, and another, and another. Where were they going? Would they ever be able to find their way back? The sailors became more and more frightened. Another long week, and still no signs of land.

"What shall we do, captain?" they asked.

"Sail on and on!" was Columbus' brave answer.

9. The king and queen of Spain had promised a reward to the one who should first see land. But even this reward no longer interested the sailors. They made up their minds they would go no farther. They talked among themselves.

"Let us throw Columbus overboard," they said, "and then sail for home."

10. Just about this time some of them see birds fly over the ship. They see seaweed floating by. They see in the water a branch with berries on it. A carved stick is picked up. All these things seem to be signs that they are near land.

But most of the sailors are too discouraged to show any interest in them. They lie down in their hammocks. But they cannot sleep. Everything seems hopeless. They think of their homes and their friends whom they never expect to see again. Sadly they toss on their pillows.

11. Suddenly they start! What is *that* they hear?

"*Land! Land!*"

It is the voice of their leader.

Then they hear a gun fired!

They leap from their hammocks. They rush to the deck. They gaze with strained eyeballs out over the water. They see a faint light in the distance. *Look!* It seems to be moving from place to place. Hoping, yet hardly daring to hope, they wait for the morning.

12. When daylight came, they were near a beautiful green shore. It was the twelfth day of October, 1492, just ten weeks from the time they sailed from Spain. Columbus, dressed in a rich scarlet cloak, was the first to go ashore. He and the sailors bowed down and kissed the ground. They wept tears of joy.

They had landed on a small island near Florida. Columbus named it San Sal'va-dor. But to the day of his death, Columbus never knew that he had found a new world. He thought he had reached India, so he named the people living on the island, Indians.

This shows Columbus and his sailors landing on San Salvador. Which is Columbus? Where are the Indians? Can you find the three ships?

Comprehension Test

1. Who discovered America? When? Where did he live when he was a little boy?

2. What part of the world did people know about at that time? What parts of the world were not known? Show this on the globe or map.

3. Why were people afraid to sail away from land? What did they think was the shape of the

earth? What did Columbus think about the shape of the earth?

4. What country did he think he could reach by sailing across the ocean? How did people travel to that country then? Why did many people laugh at his ideas?

5. What king and queen helped him to get ships for the unknown voyage? What were the names of the ships? How long did it take to make the trip?

6. How did the sailors feel after they had sailed for weeks? Who first saw land? What did Columbus call the people on this land? How many years is it since Columbus landed in the New World?

An Ax to Grind (S5)

This story and the next one are for your fifth silent reading rate drill for the first period. The boys may silently read one, while the girls read the other. At the end of three minutes the teacher will call, "Mark!" Mark the place where you are reading, and go right on reading to the end of the story. Find your reading rate, and mark it on your rate graph.

After that, the girls may tell, or read aloud, their story to the boys, and the boys may tell theirs, or read it aloud, to the girls.

These stories teach lessons that all should learn. If you read the first story, find out what people mean by saying, "He had an ax to grind." If you read the second story, find out what is meant by the saying, "You paid too much for the whistle."

1. One cold morning in winter, when I was a little boy, I met a man with an ax on his shoulder.

"My pretty boy," said he, smiling, "has your father a grind′stone?"

"Yes, sir," said I.

"You are a fine little fellow," said he. "Will you let me grind my ax on it?"

2. His words of flat′ter-y made me happy, and I was glad to do anything he wanted. I told him that the grindstone was in the shop. We went to the shop.

"My little man," he said, patting me on the head, "will you get me some hot water?"

How could I refuse? I ran and soon brought it.

"How old are you? and what is your name?" he next asked me. Without waiting for me to tell him, he then said, "You

are a fine little man, the finest boy that I have ever seen. Will you turn the grindstone just a few minutes for me?"

3. All these kind words made me so very happy that I went to work with a will. It was a new ax, and I toiled and tugged till I was almost tired out. The school bell rang, but I could not get away. Soon my hands were blis′tered, and yet the ax was not half ground. But by and by the ax was sharpened.

"Be off to school, you little tru′ant,"* he then said sharply. "The teacher will punish you."

4. These words made me sad. It was hard to turn the grindstone, but to be called a truant was too much.

His words sank deep in my mind. I have thought of them many times since. I never hear a man flat′ter-ing anyone, but I think, "I know that man has an ax to grind."

Look out for flattery, boys and girls. There are many who will want you to "turn the grindstone."

Paying Too Much for a Whistle [85]

As you read this story, find out what people mean when they say, "You paid too much for the whistle." Did *you* ever pay too much for a whistle?

How far can you read in three minutes? Find your silent reading rate, and mark it on your rate graph.

---

6   When some one has spent money
14   for a foolish thing he thought he wanted,
17   people sometimes say,
24   "He paid too much for the whistle."
30   What do they mean by that?
35   Ask Benjamin Franklin. He knows.
41   When Benjamin was seven years old,
47   his mother gave him some pennies.
53   They were the first spending money
56   Benjamin ever had.
63   He felt very happy and quite rich.
71   It was a holiday, and his mother said
77   he might go to the store
82   and buy anything he pleased.
86   Off little Benjamin trotted.
94   On the way, he met a little boy
102   with a whistle. What a beauty it was!
110   So bright and shiny! And what a loud,

shrill, cheerful voice it had!
Benjamin thought nothing could be nicer than a whistle like that.
He ran to the store as fast as his little legs could carry him.
"Do you keep whistles, sir?" he asked.
"Yes, indeed! All kinds of whistles. Wooden ones and tin ones. How much do you want to pay for one?"
"I will give you all the money I have," said Benjamin, laying all his pennies on the counter.
"Take any one you like," said the man.
Benjamin looked at them.
He saw a tin one that was bright and shiny.
He blew it. Its cheerful voice just suited him.
He took it, and left the store.
"Hear my whistle!" he said to his brothers and sisters.
"How much did you pay for it?" they asked.
"I gave all the money I had. It's a beauty, isn't it?"
They all laughed at the poor little boy.

"You have paid four times
as much as it is worth," they said.

Benjamin looked at his little treasure.
"Four times as much as it is worth,"
kept ringing in his ears.
He thought how many other nice things
he might have had with some of the money.
But now it was too late.
He felt so disappointed
that he sat down and cried.
But he had learned a good lesson.

"Never mind, Ben, you will understand
how to trade the next time,"
his father said, to comfort him.
"We all have to live and learn.
I have paid too much for a whistle
more than once in my life."

Franklin

Benjamin Franklin afterwards grew
to be a great man. When he was tempted
to buy something he did not need,
he would say to himself,
"Don't pay too much for the whistle,"
and he saved his money. He often thought
he saw big men—many of them—
who "paid too much for the whistle."

Reading Tests and Scores for the First Period

1. You have now finished your reading work for the first period of school. You are ready for your first period tests. These tests will show you what your progress in reading has been during the past six weeks. Do your very best in these interesting tests.

In your *silent reading* test, remember that comprehension goes hand in hand with rate. Rate without comprehension would be like the race that the hare and the tortoise took one time. The hare represents rate, or speed, the tortoise represents comprehension. The tortoise, though slow, won the race at last. Do you know this story? If not, ask your teacher to tell it to you. Don't be slow and poky like the tortoise, nor yet swift and foolish like the hare. Try to show the good qualities of both.

2. At this time, you will also have an *oral reading* test. In taking this test you may choose any story you have had this period. Study it as much as you please. Practice on it at home if you like. When your test is given, your score should show your very best effort. What are the four things you have learned that count in oral reading?

3. Your score, or grade, in *memory reading* will depend on the amount of memory reading you have prepared well enough to recite in public in an interesting way without any help from anyone. You can find out your grade in memory reading from the standard given on pages 36 and 37.

SECOND PERIOD

The Little Dictionary Teacher

A
B
C
D

E
F
G
H

I
J
K
L

You have all heard of a dic′tion-a-ry, I suppose. Every school has one, or should have one. And every boy and girl should learn how to use it.

Most school dictionaries are too large for third grade pupils to use, so this year you are going to have a small one which will be easy to use. Turn to page 243 in the back of your reader. Here is the little dictionary for the third grade.

When you learn how to use this dictionary, you won't need to ask your teacher how to pronounce any of the new words or tell you what they mean. Your little dictionary will do that. It will be almost like a teacher, won't it? So let us call it "The Little Dictionary Teacher."

Every one in the class can have this teacher at the same time, and you won't have to wait till Ruth or Nellie or Charles or Johnny gets through asking questions. You can go to your "Little Dictionary Teacher" any time you need to, and it will answer your questions right away.

The very first thing you will need to learn is how to find *quickly* the word you want to know about. Notice carefully the words in heavy black letters on the first page of your dictionary. With what letter do they begin? *A* is the first letter of the al′pha-bet, isn't it? If in any reading lesson you should have a new word that begins with the letter *a*, you could find it right here where all the new words are that begin with *a*. It wouldn't do any good to look anywhere else for it, because all the *a* words are here.

Look down the list of *a* words until you find the very last one. With what letter does the next black word begin? *B*, of course, because *b* comes next after *a* in the alphabet.

Look through all the *b* words, and next after them you will find all the words beginning with *c*. Then all the words beginning with *d*. Then the *e* words, the *f* words, the *g* words, and so on till you get to the very end of the alphabet. Like good children, every word is always in its own place. None of them are ever out of order.

The better you know your alphabet, the more quickly you can find any word you want your "Little Dictionary Teacher" to tell you about. You will need to learn it so well that you can find any letter without stopping to think. It may help you to find words quickly if you learn them in groups as they are on the side of these pages.

See how quickly you can point to these groups of letters: MNOP, ABCD, IJKL, EFGH, UVWXYZ, EFGH, QRST, ABCD, etc.

Point to the group in which G is found; O; T; X; etc.

Point quickly to these letters: X, A, F, C, M, P, R, O, S, etc.

M
N
O
P

Q
R
S
T

U
V
W
X
Y
Z

What letter in the alphabet comes—
Just before *i*? Just after *i*?
Just before *o*? Just after *o*? etc.

Practice on these alphabet drills from time to time until you can point to the letters as fast as your teacher can name them.

Reading Drills for the Second Period[1]

Before "The Little Dictionary Teacher" can teach you how to pronounce new words, you will need to know the marks that tell the sounds of all the letters. But you know a good many of these marks already, for you learned some of them when you were in the first grade. You learned more of them when you were in the second grade, and this year you will learn them all. This period you will have all the sounds and markings of *a* and *e*. Learn them well, and learn to *use* them.

Sounds of *a*
ā, as in nāme
ă, as in ăt
ä, as in ärm
a̤, as in a̤ll
à, as in làst
a̰, as in wha̰t
â, as in câre
ã, as in westwãrd

Sounds of *e*
ē, as in mē
ĕ, as in lĕt
ẽ, as in hẽr
ḛ, as in thḛy
ḛ̂, as in thḛ̂ir

---
[1] TO THE TEACHER: Before giving these drills, read the suggestions for teachers in "To the Teacher" under the topic, "Reading Drills" in the section "Reading, Grades Three and Four" of the "Teacher's Handbook on the Elementary Curriculum."

Polite Away From Home [O]

Was the boy in this story truly polite? How do you think a polite child should act at home?

As you read orally, notice the words that are printed in italics. They will help you to read as the people in the story spoke. Mark off the phrases in the first section with short cross lines. This will help you to read easily and smoothly, and also to look away from your book to your audience without losing your place.

---

1. Charles Butler was on his way to school. A lady opened a window, and called to him.

"Charlie! I wonder if I could get you to mail this letter for me? Are you going near the post office?"

"Yes, Mrs. Ross, near enough to run over and mail your letter," said Charlie, as he lifted his hat to the lady.

"I don't want to make you late to school," said Mrs. Ross; "but if you *can* take the letter to the office, I shall be *very* much obliged."

"Oh, there's no danger of being late!" replied Charlie. "It will take only a minute to run around the corner to the office." And as he received the letter, he politely lifted his hat again.

2. "What a *perfect* little *gentleman* that Charlie Butler is!" said Mrs. Ross to her husband as she closed the window. "He is always *so obliging.** He acts just as if it were a *great pleasure* to do a favor."

3. Now that was all very nice in Charlie, but let me tell you something else. Not more than five minutes before Mrs. Ross called him, his mother had said, "Charlie, can't you run upstairs, please, and get that letter on my bureau* and mail it for me?"

And Charlie, with a frown on his forehead and a pucker on each side of his mouth, had said, "Oh, *mamma!* I don't see how I *can.* I am late *now*, and the office is *half a block* out of my way."

"Well, then, you need not mind," said his mother, for she did not want him to be late to school. So he didn't mind, but left the letter on the bureau, and went briskly on his way until stopped by Mrs. Ross.

4. What was the matter with Charlie? Was he an untruthful boy? He did not mean to be. He claimed to be strictly honest. It was growing late, and he felt in a hurry, and he did not want to go upstairs.

Of *course*, it would not do to refuse *Mrs. Ross*. And, by making an extra rush, he *could* get to school in time. But the *other* lady was only his *mother*. *Her* letter could wait.

Only his mother! Didn't Charlie love his mother, then? You ask him, with a hint of doubt about it in your voice, and see how his eyes will flash, and how he will toss his head, and say, "Indeed, I *do* love my mother! She is the *best* mother a boy ever had!"

5. I did not promise to explain Charlie's conduct to you. I am only introducing* him. You are to study the cause of his action for yourself. Do you know any boy like him? Maybe you know a girl that does as he did.

—*Pansy.**

Proverbs of Solomon [o]

Ask your "Dictionary Teacher" what a proverb is. Who was Solomon? How many proverbs did he speak? 1 Kings 4:32 tells. How did he become so wise? 1 Kings 4:29 tells.

---

1. A wise son maketh a glad father:
   But a foolish son
   is the heaviness* of his mother.

2. A false balance*
   is abomination* to the Lord:
   But a just weight is His delight.

Lincoln said, "I will study and get ready."

3. He that turneth away his ear
   from hearing the law,
   Even his prayer shall be abomination.

4. A good name is rather to be chosen than great riches,
   And loving favor
   rather than silver and gold.

5. Even a child
   is known by his doings,
   Whether his work be pure,
   and whether it be right.

—*The Bible.*

1. "The heaviness of his mother" means a mother with a heavy or very sad heart.

2. A "false balance" means not weighing things honestly that we expect to sell. God hates such dishonesty. It is abomination to Him. Can you tell what "a just weight" is?

3. God cannot listen to the prayer of one who will not obey Him. The prayer of such a person is not a real prayer. God hates, or abominates, such a prayer.

4. "A good name" means a good life, or character.

5. Which proverb in this lesson do you like best?

"Give Us This Day Our Daily Bread" (S)

This story and the next one tell how God has answered prayer. Study the one the teacher gives you until you understand it. Then read or tell it to the other pupils in such a way that they will enjoy listening to you.

How long does it take you to read silently the story given you?

Two words in this story have a star after them. Find them, and ask your "Dictionary Teacher" what they mean. Practice reading paragraphs one and two orally.

1. Johnny Hall was a poor boy. His mother worked hard for their daily bread.

"Mother, please give me something to eat; I am hungry," he said one evening.

His mother let the work upon which she was sewing fall from her knee, as she drew Johnny toward her.

2. "Mother is very poor, and cannot give you any supper to-night," she said, as her tears fell fast.

"Oh, never mind, mother, I shall soon be asleep, and then I shall not feel hungry. But you will sit and sew, and be so hungry and cold. Poor mother!" he said, and kissed her many times to comfort her.

3. Before Johnny went to bed, he and his mother repeated "The Lord's Prayer" together. "Our Father," they prayed until they came to the petition,* "Give us this day our daily bread."

Johnny noticed the earnestness, almost agony, with which his mother spoke these words. He said them over again: "Give us this day our daily bread." Then, opening his blue eyes, he fixed them on his mother, and said, "We shall never be hungry any more. God is *our Father*, and He will hear our prayer."

4. The prayer was finished, and Johnny went to rest. The mother sewed on far into the night. Her heart was made happy by the faith of her child. Many promises came to her mind. Although she was tired and hungry, still it was with a light heart that she went to rest at last.

Early in the morning, a gentleman called on his way to business. He asked Johnny's mother to come to his home to take care of his two motherless* boys. She knew that in this way God had answered their prayer. They were given all the comforts of a good home. Johnny is a big man now, but he has never forgotten that time when he prayed so earnestly for his daily bread. He still believes that God will hear our prayers.

The Prayer of a Poor Woman [S]

1. One winter morning,
a Christian lady
who had often given to the poor,
sat alone in her room.
Soon, her daughter came in.
"My dear, old Mr. and Mrs. Wood
have been in my mind all night.
I hear that they are very poor.
They may be sick and in need.
I wish you would take a basket to the city
and buy some food and take it to them."

As her daughter was leaving the room,
the lady handed her a thick flannel skirt.
"Perhaps it would be well to take this, too,"
she said. "The weather is cold,
and Mrs. Wood may need it."

2. The daughter went.
The food was bought,
and at the head of the third flight of stairs
in the house where Mr. and Mrs. Wood lived,
she stopped. Through the door she heard
Mr. Wood's voice asking God's blessing
upon the food before him.

When he had finished,
she knocked and entered.
Sure enough, there they were at dinner,
the wife at the foot of the table,
waiting to be helped,
the husband at the head, cutting—
one large apple!
This was all the food they had!

3. With tears in her eyes,
the daughter drew forth her kindly stores,
and while a comfortable meal
was being made ready
she listened to their grateful thanks.

They told her how they had fallen sick
and had not been able to work,
and so had been left in great need.
They had told God all their troubles,
and they believed He would send them help.

4. When dinner was ready,
and the visitor was about to leave,
Mrs. Wood went with her to the door.
"My dear, did you bring the flannel skirt?"
she asked.

In the excitement of getting the dinner,

the daughter had quite forgotten the skirt
that lay in the bottom of the basket.

"Yes, I brought you a skirt;
but why do you think so?"
she asked in surprise.

"Because, dear," said the woman,
"when I told the Lord
that there was only one apple left,
I told Him I needed a warm flannel skirt,
and I was wondering whether you had it,
or whether He would send it
by some one else."

Towser and the Chicks (S1)

This story is your first silent reading rate drill for the second period. See how much you can read in three minutes. Then see how well you can tell the story to the rest of the class. How many starred words in this story? In every lesson after this, if there are any starred words that you do not understand, ask your "Dictionary Teacher" what they mean.

₈ Towser was a fine fluffy poodle dog. His
₁₆ bed was in a kennel* carpeted with straw.
₂₃ One evening, he saw something round and
₃₂ white and smooth lying in one corner of his

kennel. Towser was a good dog, so he did not meddle with it. He lay down and went to sleep. The next night there was another, and then another, and another, until thirteen lay in the corner together.

Then, on the fourteenth night, Towser found something else in his kennel. It was a little bantam* hen covering the round, white eggs with her body and wings.

Towser and the bantam were the best of friends. They often ate out of the same dish. I think Towser felt pleased to have the bantam choose his kennel for her nest. He lay with his nose just a little nearer the door of his kennel, that he might better guard his little friend.

Every night for just three weeks, Towser found the bantam snuggled in one corner of his kennel. On the twenty-first night, he heard strange sounds. There were faint "peeps," the cracking of eggshells, and the soft "cluck" of the bantam hen.

Towser could not understand what was going on. But it made him wakeful, and he

Doesn't Towser make a soft, warm bed for the motherless chicks?

pricked up his ears and barked a little. The next day, he saw his little friend walking about the yard with eleven little chickens. He was delighted! He frisked about the hen, and showed his joy in other ways.

A week later, the poor little mother hen was run over and killed. Then Towser took the chicks into his kennel, and lay down in the corner. They snuggled close up under the long hair of his body. He lay very quiet.

He did not want to disturb or injure them. In that way he took care of them all night. The next day, he led them out into the yard. He barked at them with delight. He scratched the ground till it was nice and soft. Then the little chicks would scratch for themselves in the soft earth.

It was a funny sight to see Towser going about the yard followed by the little chicks. But Towser took care of them until they were large enough to take care of themselves. —*Christian Work.*

Comprehension Test. Read the following sentences one at a time. Decide which word or phrase in the parenthesis* ( ) makes the sentence true. Then draw a line under that word or phrase.

1. Towser was a (Newfoundland, shepherd, poodle) dog.
2. The bantam hen laid (three, ten, thirteen) eggs in his kennel.
3. Towser and the bantam were (friends, enemies).
4. The eggs hatched in (fourteen, twenty-one, ten) days.
5. One day (Towser, the bantam, a baby chick) was killed.

Daisies [80]

A poet can paint beautiful pictures with words because he sees beauty in everything he writes about. Mr. Sherman has painted some very pretty word pictures in this poem. What picture can you find in the first stanza? in the second stanza? in the third stanza?

At evening when I go to bed,
I see the stars shine overhead.
They are the little daisies white
That dot the meadows* of the night.

And often, while I'm dreaming so,
Across the sky the moon will go.
She is a lady, sweet and fair,
Who comes to gather daisies there.

For, when at morning I arise,
There's not a star left in the skies.
She's picked them all,
    and dropped them down
Into the meadows of the town.

—*Frank Dempster Sherman.*

Clouds [139]

Each stanza of this poem has a beautiful word picture. Try to see it.

Read stanza 1. What time of day does this stanza tell about? What are the clouds like? Can you think why the wind is like the shepherd boys? What do the shepherd boys drive? What do the winds drive?

Read stanza 2. What time of day does this stanza tell about? What color do the clouds make the sky? Where have the winds driven the clouds? Draw and color this picture as it looks to you.

Read stanza 3. What time of day does this stanza tell about? What are the stars like? What are the "shadow bars"? What does the wind say to his sheep?

---

1. The sky is full of clouds to-day,
   And idly to and fro,
   Like sheep across the pasture, they
   Across the heavens go.
   I hear the wind with merry* noise
   Around the housetops sweep,
   And dream it is the shepherd boys—
   They're driving home their sheep.

2. The clouds move faster now, and see!
   The west is red and gold;
   Each sheep seems hastening to be
   The first within the fold.*
   I watch them hurry on until
   The blue is clear and deep,
   And dream that far beyond the hill
   The shepherds fold* their sheep.

3. Then in the sky the trembling stars
   Like little flowers shine out,
   While night puts up the shadow bars,
   And darkness falls about.
   I hear the shepherd wind's "Good-night,—
   Good-night and happy sleep!"
   And dream that in the east, all white,
   Slumber the clouds,—the sheep.
   —*Frank Dempster Sherman.*

The Fly [O]

1. Baby-bye,
   Here's a fly;
   Let us watch him, you and I.
   How he crawls
   Up the walls,
   Yet he never falls!

I believe with six such legs
You and I could walk on eggs.
   There he goes
   On his toes,
   Tickling baby's nose.

2. Spots of red
   Dot his head;
Rainbows on his back are spread;
   That small speck
   Is his neck;
   See him nod and beck!
I can show you, if you choose,
Where to look for his wee* shoes,
   Three small pairs,
   Made of hairs;
   These he always wears.

3. Flies can see
   More than we;
So how bright their eyes must be!
   Little fly,
   Ope* your eye;
   Spiders are near by.

For a secret I can tell,
Spiders never use flies well;
Then away,
Do not stay,
Little fly, good day.

—*Author Unknown.*

Comprehension Test
1. How many legs does a fly have?
2. Did you ever see the "spots of red" on a fly's head?
3. Did you ever see the "rainbow" on his back?
4. How large is his neck?
5. How many pairs of shoes does he wear? What are they made of?

Things to Find Out
1. Why can a fly see more than you can?
2. What do spiders do to flies?

Half an Apple (o)

As you read this story orally, try to make your voice sound as you think the people in the story spoke. Think of something that *you* could do to be kind to a new pupil. What word is starred? Do you know its meaning?

One cold morning, a number of girls and boys were gathered around the stove in a schoolroom. They talked and laughed among themselves. A new pupil stood apart from the rest. Now and then the children looked at her, but no one spoke to her.

The little girl had never been to that school before. She felt shy and homesick. She wished she could run home to mother, and have a good cry in her loving arms. One little teardrop trembled in her eye, and seemed ready to fall. But it never did, for just then something happened.

Suddenly, the outside door flew open, and a bright-eyed, rosy-cheeked little girl rushed in. She brought plenty of the clear, frosty air with her. She brought a cheer to the schoolroom, too, that it had not had before. She walked up to the stove quite as if she were at home. After saying "Good morning" to every one, her eyes fell upon the new pupil.

"Good morning," she sweetly said across the stovepipe.

The little girl on the other side brightened up at once, though she answered somewhat timidly.

"Cold, is it not?" the newcomer went on, pulling off her mittens, and holding her red hands over the stove. Then she sent one of her plump hands down into the depths of her pocket, and when it came out, it held a fine, red apple. With her strong fingers she split it in two, and with a smile, passed half of it to the new pupil.

"Do you like apples?" she asked.

The little girl did like apples very much, and she thought none had ever tasted half so good as this; it was so juicy and crisp and tart.*

"My name is Libby," said the owner of the bright eyes. "What is your name?"

"My name is Hetty," replied the new little girl.

"Well," said Libby, "do you want to sit with me? No one sits in the seat beside mine, and I know the teacher will let you."

Hetty thought she would like that plan very much. So the two girls went to find Libby's seat. There they chatted happily till the bell rang.

"Where is Hetty Rowe?" asked the teacher.

Then, before anyone had time to answer, she saw her seated next to merry-faced Libby.

"I see you are in good hands," said the kind teacher, smiling.

When Libby had grown to be a woman, she told me the story herself. She used to say that it was her gift of half an apple that won for her so dear a friend as Hetty Rowe.

But I think it was something besides the apple that comforted the sad little heart on that cold morning, don't you?

—Selected.

Comprehension Test. Draw a line under the word or words in the parenthesis ( ) that makes the sentence true.

1. The schoolroom was heated by (stove, furnace, gas).
2. The new pupil felt (happy, homesick, shy).
3. Her name was (Hetty, Libby).
4. One of the girls gave her an (orange, apple, peach).
5. (The fruit, the girl's kindness, the teacher) comforted the new pupil.

Old Tusky [S]

Read this story silently, and find out who Old Tusky was, and where he lived. What shows that elephants are affectionate? Make a list of all the things about elephants that you knew before. Make another list of the things that you did not know.

There are five starred words in this story. Can you pronounce them correctly? Guess their meaning and then ask your "Dictionary Teacher" if you guessed right.

Tusky was the name of a big elephant. He lived in Burma. He was as fine an elephant as you could ever see. Such a giant was he! And such beautiful ivory tusks! Best of all, he was such a wise, knowing beast!

Most elephants live to be about eighty years of age, and a few of them live to be one hundred years old. I suppose Tusky was at least eighty years old.

One day two men went to take a picture of Tusky. They found him lying down. There was something the matter with his feet. They seemed to be rotting away. A few days after this, poor old Tusky died.

About half an hour before he died, he

went totally blind. He dearly loved his keeper, and when he could no longer see him, he became very restless. He kept feeling all about with his trunk.

At last his keeper stepped close to him. He gently patted the poor sick animal.

"What do you want, Tusky?" he asked kindly.

Of course, Tusky could not talk, but he knew his master's voice. He just wrapped his trunk around his master and drew him close up in a loving embrace.* There the man was held until the elephant breathed his last. The keeper cried like a child. And every one who saw dear old Tusky die, wept.

When Tusky was a baby, he was about as large as the largest dog you ever saw. When he was full grown, he was at least ten feet high. He weighed about as much as six very large horses.

In India and Burma elephants are taught to work. Sometimes they work in lumber camps. An elephant can lift heavy logs. He carries them on his tusks, and holds them there by wrapping his long trunk about them. If a log is too heavy to carry, he will take hold of one end and drag it to its place.

An elephant can also learn to push or pull a wagon. He can push better than he can pull. He can even push a car on a railroad track.

In India men sometimes hunt tigers from the back of an elephant. A long time ago soldiers used elephants in war. The elephants would stamp the enemy underfoot. After a while the enemy learned that they could frighten the huge beasts away by waving burning torches* before them.

These elephants live in Burma. How well they are piling the heavy logs!

HERBERT PHOTO

This is Junior Jumbo. He lives in a New York park. How would you like a ride on his back? Do you see the far-away look in his eyes? Is he thinking of his old home in India, I wonder?

Jumbo was the name of a very large elephant in the London Zoo. One time, a man wanted to buy Jumbo. How much do you think he paid for him? A hundred dollars? A thousand dollars? How much? He paid ten thousand dollars to get him!

Once the school children in St. Louis wanted to get an elephant to put in the city zoo. They all saved their pennies. When they had enough to make $2,385, they bought an elephant. They named him Jim. If you are ever in St. Louis, you may see Jim in the zoo.

In India people ride on elephants. The seat is tied on the elephant's back. It is called a howdah.* How do you suppose people get into the howdah? Usually they climb up by using a ladder. Or the elephant may kneel. Sometimes an elephant will lift one of his forefeet and bend it upward. Then the rider steps on the elephant's foot, seizes him by the ear, and climbs into the howdah.

A Howdah

An elephant is a very affectionate* animal. He will love and protect anyone who treats him kindly. Even on this earth he can be taught to do many things. But in the new earth he will be even more intelligent* and gentle.

Comprehension Test. Read these sentences, and choose the word or phrase in the parenthesis that makes the sentence true.

1. Most elephants live to be (eighty, one hundred) years old.
2. A baby elephant is about as large as a big (cat, dog, horse).
3. A full-grown elephant is at least (ten, twenty) feet high.
4. He weighs as much as (six, three) very large horses.
5. An elephant carries logs on his (back, tusks).

Answer These Questions Correctly:

1. In what countries are elephants taught to work? Find these places on the map on page xi.
2. What else are they used for?
3. Where is there a school children's elephant? Locate the city on the map on page xii.
4. How can a person get on an elephant's back?
5. How will the elephants in the new earth differ from those here?

Diamond (S2)

This story is your second silent reading drill for the second period. Find your rate, and mark it on your rate graph. It is also a fine story to read orally to others.

Diamond was a heathen boy who became a Christian. As you read about him, find out what he did which showed that he was a real Christian. Find his home on the globe or on the map of Asia.

---

8 Diamond is a boy who lives in far-away
16 India. Like millions of others in India, his
24 people are heathen. They do not know the
32 true God. They do not know that Jesus
37 loves them. They worship idols.
44 One day, Diamond heard about our mis-
52 sion school. He heard that at the school he
60 could learn of Jesus. But the school was
68 hundreds of miles away. He made up his
77 mind to go to the mission school. Day after
82 day, he thought about it.
91 At last he left his home, and made his
100 way to the school. After he had been at
108 the school a few weeks, his parents tried
114 to compel him to return home.
122 Those at the school feared that if he

went home he would go back to his old heathen ways. They loved Diamond, and wanted him to be a true child of God. They hoped he would stay at the school. Diamond stayed a few days longer. But then he felt that he ought to return home.

"Sahib,* I must go," he said to the one in charge of the mission.

And he went. The missionaries thought that, as he had been with them only a few weeks, he would now give up all thought of being a Christian.

A few weeks later, the missionary received a letter from Diamond. The boy begged him to come down and visit him at his home. He said that he had been suffering persecution* for the truth's sake. He longed to have the missionary pray with him and encourage him.

The missionary was very busy, and it was difficult for him to leave. But he wanted to help Diamond, so he went. He traveled three hundred miles by train, and crossed eleven rivers, some of which were very deep.

When he found Diamond, he talked with him and prayed with him. He encouraged him to be true and faithful to God.

The boy told the missionary about his troubles. At first his people tried to persuade him to give up Jesus. When he refused, they put his Bible and all his other things in a box. Then they sank the box in a well.

After a while, Diamond found it and pulled it out. First of all, he took from it his Bible. He carefully turned its pages in the heat of the sun, and dried them so he might again read God's word. He had learned to love the great and precious promises that God had given him.

Diamond took the missionary into the village. He showed him a little shack—just a simple little mud building with a thatched* roof.

"What is that, Diamond?" the missionary asked.

What do you suppose that little shack was? It was Diamond's schoolhouse! When

Diamond's schoolhouse was something like this. Do you see the thatched roof?

he had to leave the mission school, he decided to have a little mission school of his own. So he talked to the boys of the village about it. They became interested, and together they had built the little schoolhouse. There, day by day, forty boys and girls of the village came to be taught about Jesus, the children's Friend. And Diamond was the teacher!

Diamond had studied the Bible only a few weeks in the mission school. He was a poor, ignorant boy, but he was a real diamond in the rough. The Lord took him, and made him a true missionary to the other boys and girls in his town.

Boys and girls in our church schools, you have the privilege of studying the Bible year after year. What are you planning to do with the wonderful Bible knowledge that you are storing in your minds?

Comprehension Test
1. In what country does Diamond live?
2. Where did he go to learn about Jesus?
3. After he had been there a few weeks, where did he go?
4. A few weeks later, what did he ask the missionary to do?
5. How far did Diamond live from the mission?
6. How did Diamond's people persecute him?
7. What did Diamond do to help his people?
8. How many boys and girls attended this school?
9. Who was the teacher?
10. What were the pupils taught?

Mary's Lamb ^(o)

Mary and her little lamb lived many years ago near Boston. As you read, find out why the lamb loved Mary.

---

1. Mary had a little lamb,
    His fleece* was white as snow,—
   And everywhere that Mary went,
    That lamb was sure to go.

2. He followed her to school one day,—
    That was against the rule;
   It made the children laugh and play,
    To see a lamb at school.

3. And so the teacher turned him out,
    But still he lingered* near,
   And waited patiently about,
    Till Mary did appear.*

4. And then he ran to her and laid
    His head upon her arm,
   As if to say, "I'm not afraid,—
    You'll keep me from all harm."

5. "What makes the lamb
    love Mary so?"
   The eager* children cry.
   "Oh! Mary loves the lamb,
    you know,"
   The teacher did reply.
   —*Sarah J. Hale.*

The Raindrops' Journey [83]

1. Some little drops of water,
    Whose home was in the sea,
   To go upon a journey
    Once happened to agree.

2. A cloud they had for carriage;
    They drove a playful breeze,
   And over town and country
    They rode along at ease.

3. But oh, there were *so many*,
    At last the carriage broke,
   And to the ground came tumbling
    These happy little folk.

4. And through the moss and grasses
    They were compelled to roam,
   Until a brooklet* found them,
    And carried them all home.

—*Author Unknown.*

Things to Find Out
1. How did the raindrops get into the cloud?
2. What caused them to fall from the cloud?
3. All brooklets and rivers flow into the sea. Then why does not the sea get too full and overflow?
4. Tell the five steps in the journey of the raindrops.

A Little Girl Whom God Used (S)

This is a good story to practice on till you can read it well to some one else. As you read it, decide what part you think is the most interesting. What part makes you feel sad? Time yourself, and see how long it takes to read the whole story silently.

1. Ellen Harmon is the name of a little twin girl who was born in Maine, a little more than a century* ago. Her twin sister's name was Elizabeth. These baby twins had six other brothers and sisters. The father and mother were earnest Christians, and all the children became Christians.

2. These children were taught to reverence God, and to respect their parents. They were taught to be honest and truthful. They were taught to do their share of the work about the home. They were also taught to help the poor about them. They were taught to obey the laws of health, so there was very little sickness in the family.

3. Ellen was a happy little baby, the very picture of health, and she soon grew to be a strong, joyous little girl. She spread sun-

shine wherever she went. While she was still a child, she loved to study. She understood quickly, and she had a very good memory. If she had a difficult lesson to learn or some hard work to do, she did not give up until the thing was done. Her parents were glad to see their little daughter love that which was right. They hoped she would become a useful, noble woman.

4. One day, when Ellen was nine years old, she was going home from school with Elizabeth and one of their schoolmates. Another girl who was angry about something was following them and trying to strike them. Ellen's mother had taught her children never to quarrel, but if anyone was trying to hurt them, to run home as fast as they could. So the girls hurried on.

5. The angry girl hurried, too, to keep up with them. Ellen turned her head to see how far behind her the angry girl was. Just then, the girl threw a stone, and hit little Ellen a terrible blow on the nose. Ellen dropped to the ground, unconscious!*

6. The girls were all greatly frightened as they saw the blood streaming from her nose. The next thing Ellen knew, she was lying in a store near by, the floor and her garments covered with blood. After a time she tried to walk home, but she grew faint and dizzy. So her twin sister and her schoolmate carried her home.

7. For three weeks she lay in her little bed, not knowing anything that was going on about her. Every one thought that she would die, but her mother felt that she would live. Tenderly her mother cared for her week after week. Ellen gained strength very slowly, but she never gained back her health.

8. Her father was away from home when all this happened. When he returned, he kissed all the other children, then looked around for Ellen.

"Where is my little Ellen?" he asked.

"Here she is," said her mother.

The father looked at his child, but she was so changed that he did not know her.

Her nose was broken, and her face pale and thin. It was hard to believe that this was his little Ellen whom he had left only a few months before, a healthy, happy child. Ellen tried to look cheerful, but her little heart seemed breaking. She was no longer the beautiful child she had once been, and many of her girl friends left her.

9. After this she could not attend school very much, and the education she longed for she had to go without. To her, life seemed hardly worth living, and she wished that she could die. When the thought came to her that she was not ready to die, she prayed that God would make her ready.

10. When Ellen was thirteen years old, she heard William Miller preach. He told the people that Jesus was soon coming to this earth. He told them to turn from sin and get ready to meet Him. Oh, how Ellen longed to be ready! But she was afraid she could never be a child of God. If she had only talked it all over with her mother! But the little girl kept all these feelings in her

own heart, and her mother never dreamed how unhappy Ellen was.

11. Jesus loved this child, even though she did not know it. But as she prayed and confessed her sins, one day her burden left her. Jesus seemed very near to her, and oh, how happy she was! She had taken all her sorrow to Him, and He understood and sympathized with her.

12. As she went home from meeting that day, all nature seemed changed. The sun shone more brightly, the grass seemed a fresher green, the sky a deeper blue. The trees were more beautiful, and the birds sang more sweetly. Everything seemed to be praising God. As she touched the delicate petals* of the flowers, she thought, "If God so loves and cares for the flowers, how much more will He care for me. I am a child of God! I will love Him, and obey Him, and never displease Him!"

13. After this, Ellen was baptized and joined the church. Then she tried to help other girls, for she wanted every one to be

Ellen G. White

as happy as she was. She held little prayer meetings with her young friends. These girls earned money to buy tracts to give away so that others might know about the coming of Jesus. Ellen knit stockings for twenty-five cents a pair for this work. Her father was a hatter, and, propped up in bed, Ellen made crowns for the hats. In this way she earned twenty cents a day. And she gave it all to the work of God.

14. When Ellen grew to womanhood, she married Elder James White, and then her

name became Ellen G. White. The Lord often talked to her as He did to Abraham, and Daniel, and Paul, and others that the Bible tells about. She wrote many books in which she told others what God had told her.

15. She traveled in Europe and Australia and other places, telling the people to get ready for the coming of Jesus. She loved children, and tried to encourage them to give their hearts to the Saviour. She lived a long and useful life, and helped thousands of people to love the Lord.

Speed Test. See how quickly you can find the paragraphs that answer the first eight questions.
1. What shows that Ellen was an obedient girl?
2. What was she taught at home?
3. What shows that it is always best to tell our mothers all our troubles?
4. Who was William Miller?
5. In what year did Ellen first hear him preach? Do you know what took place four years after this?
6. What shows that Ellen was really converted?
7. In what countries did she travel? Find these places on the map.
8. How did God often speak to her?
9. She was born Nov. 26, 1827, and died July 16, 1915. How old was she when she died?

Joe Black [S3]

Read this story silently for your third rate drill for this period. Then read it until you can tell it well in class. Find out how Joe showed that he was forgiving and good-natured.

Joe Black stood on the walk in front of the house where he lived. He had a coat on, but no hat.

A number of boys were out on the sidewalk. Joe was watching them play. Some of them were sliding on the ice in the gutter.* Others were snowballing. All were having a fine time.

Pretty soon, a man came along with a heavy bundle on his shoulder. Joe did not see him or hear him until he was quite near.

"Get out of my way!" he called out angrily to Joe.

Joe was frightened at the harsh tone in which the man spoke. He ran out of the way as fast as he could.

The next morning Joe was standing on the doorstep, looking up and down the street. The same man came along. He had what looked like the same bundle on his shoulder. He did not see Joe, but Joe saw him and knew him.

Joe stood still and watched him go by. Joe saw him pull his handkerchief out of his pocket. As he did so, he pulled out one of his mittens. It fell on the sidewalk. When he put his handkerchief back into his pocket, he did not miss the mitten. There it lay just where it fell.

Joe Black saw the mitten. He ran down the steps and along the walk until he came to it. He picked it up, and ran after the man as fast as his legs could carry him.

He did not call out, but waited until he was close behind the man. He then gently touched his coat.

The man turned around to see who had

touched him. There stood Joe holding up the mitten.

"Well done!" said the man, feeling in his pocket. "Where did you find that?" He took the mitten and put it into his pocket.

Joe wagged his tail. He was only a great Newfoundland* dog, and he could not speak a word.

I think Joe knew how to return good for evil. Do you not think so?

—*Gordon Third Reader.*

A fine Newfoundland dog. Doesn't he look friendly?

Obedience [42]

The ladies who wrote the two poems on this page were sisters. What lesson does each poem teach you?

Phœbe Cary

If you're told to do a thing,
    And mean to do it really;
Never let it be by halves,
    Do it fully, freely!

Do not make a poor excuse,
    Waiting, weak, unsteady;
All obedience worth the name,
    Must be prompt* and ready.
        —*Phœbe Cary.*

Alice Cary

What to Look For [52]

Do not look for wrong and evil—
    You will find them if you do;
As you measure for your neighbor,
    He will measure back to you.

Look for goodness, look for gladness,
    You will meet them all the while;
If you bring a smiling visage*
    To the glass, you meet a smile.
        —*Alice Cary.*

Robert Bruce and the Spider [S]

This story and the next one teach the same lesson. Read both stories silently, and find out what this lesson is. Have *you* ever learned any lesson from an ant or a spider? Can you guess the meaning of the four starred words? Prove your guess from the "Dictionary Teacher."

Find Scotland, England, and Asia on the globe, or on the map on page xi.

More than six hundred years ago, the people of Scotland made up their minds that they did not want to be ruled by the king of England. They wanted to rule themselves. This led to war between the two countries.

Again and again, the English army defeated* the Scotch.* At last, Robert Bruce was made leader of the Scotch army. Six times Bruce led his brave little army against the great army of England. Six times he was driven back. Then his army was scattered, and he had to hide in order to save his life.

Sometimes he hid in the woods. Sometimes he hid in the mountains, and sometimes in the huts* of poor peasants.* The English soldiers tried to find and capture him. He had to flee from one hiding place to another.

At last he was almost ready to give up. It seemed to him there was no use trying to do anything more. That night he lay down on a heap of straw in an old hut. But he could not sleep. He was thinking about his failures.

At last morning came. As he lay on his bed of straw, he was greatly discouraged. Would his country ever be free?

Just then he saw a spider trying to swing herself by her thread from one beam of the roof to another. She failed, and the thread swung back to its starting place. She tried again, and again it fell back. She made another effort, only to fall back a third time. But the little spider had started to weave a web, and she never thought of giving up. Six times she tried to throw her frail thread across. Six times it fell short.

For a moment Robert Bruce seemed to forget about his own failures. He watched the little spider with deep interest. He hoped she would not give up. He wanted to see her succeed.

The seventh time she swung herself out on her slender line. Would she fail again? No! This time the thread was thrown safely across, and fastened to the beam.

Bruce was almost ashamed of himself. If a little spider would not give up, why should he? He, too, would try the seventh time. With new courage he left his hiding place. He got his friends together. He told them of his plans. He sent them out to encourage his soldiers.

Soon another army of brave Scotchmen were around him. Another great battle was fought, and this time the English were completely defeated. They fled into their own country. Scotland was made free, and Robert Bruce was its king.

Timour and the Ant (S)

Ti′mour was a famous chief in Asia. His enemies were on his track. If they caught him, they were going to kill him. To save his life, he hid in a lonely building in the wilderness. He was sad and discouraged. It seemed to him that his load was heavier than he could bear. He did not know what to do. He felt like giving up in despair.

As he sat in the rude hut looking at the bare walls, he saw a little ant trying to carry a grain of wheat up the wall. The wheat was larger than the ant. It seemed too heavy for the tiny insect to pull up the steep wall.

Timour watched the little worker. Up the wall it slowly struggled with its heavy load. It had not gone far when the grain of wheat fell to the floor. Quickly the little ant came down the wall. It seized the wheat and started up again. But the load was too heavy, and again it dropped back to the floor.

Was the ant discouraged? Oh no! Down

it came again for its prize. Time after time the load proved too much for the little creature. Sixty-nine times Timour saw the grain fall to the floor. Sixty-nine times he watched the determined little ant return to its task. But the seventieth time it carried its load successfully!

"I was in despair," said the chief, "but the plucky* little ant gave me new courage, and I have never forgotten the noble lesson it taught me."

The Bible says:

"Go to the ant, thou sluggard,*
Consider* her ways, and be wise."

Grace Darling [S]

This story says that Grace Darling was a truly noble girl. Read the story, and see if you can find out why.

Grace Darling was the daughter of a lighthouse keeper. The lighthouse where Grace lived was on the northeast coast of England.

Grace could not remember the time when she had not been near the ocean, and she felt no more fear of it than you do of the land. When she was but a little child, her father often took her in his boat with him. As she grew older, she would sometimes row the boat. In this way she learned to handle a boat with great skill.

One night, there was a terrible storm at sea. The fog was so thick that the light in the tower could hardly be seen. During the night, a vessel was driven against the rocks and dashed in pieces. Many were drowned, but nine of the crew* were left clinging to the wreck.*

Grace had been anxious and troubled all night. As soon as it was light, she took her spy-glass,* and as she looked through it, she saw the poor men on the rocks.

"O father!" she cried, "there is a wreck on the rocks, and some of the crew are still alive!"

"Alas, poor souls, they haven't long to live," was the reply.

Grace begged her father to start out in his boat, and try to save the poor men clinging to the rocks.

"But, Grace," said he, "no boat could live in such a sea as that."

"Let me go with you, father. I can handle *one* oar."

At last the father promised to go. The noble mother helped to start the boat. As she anxiously* watched it tossing among the waves, she prayed that He "who hath measured the waters in the hollow of His hand," and who, when on earth, had stilled the tempest by a word, would take care of her loved ones.

Often the little boat sank quite out of sight, but each time it rose again. It came nearer and nearer to the wreck. The mile between the lighthouse and the steamer

was at last passed, and nine people, nearly dead with fright and cold, were helped into the little boat and brought safely to the lighthouse.

The story of this brave deed was soon told all over the world. Grace was astonished to receive costly presents for doing what she felt was only her duty. She had not braved that awful storm for the sake of being known and admired. Her whole desire was to save those who without help would surely have perished.* And it is this unselfish desire that makes her deed truly noble.

It is now nearly one hundred years since Grace Darling risked her life to save others. Though she is now dead, the influence* of her unselfish thought for others still lives. She lies buried in the little churchyard by the sea, not far from her old home. The monument placed in honor of the brave girl is a figure carved in stone of a woman lying at rest, with a boat's oar held fast in her right hand.

We cannot all show our courage in the same way that Grace did; but we may in other ways, if we are not cowards. Courage is needed in little things as well as in great. In time of accident or sickness, brave people bear suffering without complaining. A boy or a girl who has courage will never give up a task because it is hard.

It often takes courage to tell the truth. It takes courage to do right at all times. When refused what we very much wish, it takes courage to bear the disappointment with patience. Whether we ever have a chance to do *great*, brave deeds or not, we can show our courage just as much by being brave in *little* things.

Something to Study

1. The storm that this story tells about was on the ocean near a small island off the northeast coast of England. This island is called Farne, or Fern, Island. Find England and Farne Island on the map or globe. Which way on the map is north? east? northeast? Point to the other directions on a map. Point in the direction of England.

2. Grace Darling was born in the year 1815. This storm was in 1838. How old was Grace then?

3. When she died, what monument was made for her?

4. This story names four *little* things that take courage? What are they? Can you think of any other little thing that takes courage?

Match each picture with the paragraph in the story that tells about it.

A Fawn Saved From Dogs (S4)

Does a fawn talk? This one did. Find out from this story what she said and how she said it. Find your silent reading rate, and mark it on your rate graph. Practice reading the last paragraph orally.

1. It was a beautiful summer day in a western forest.* A handsome fawn* lay in an open place. She had eaten a good breakfast of leaves and grass, and was lying down, enjoying the pleasant sunshine. The flowers were peeping up all about her. Above her the birds were singing sweetly in the trees. Far beyond, the quiet clouds floated in the blue sky.

2. All at once a strange sound came through the forest. It startled the gentle fawn, and she quickly sprang to her feet. It was the barking of dogs. She knew they were on her track, and that she must flee at once for her life.

Off she started at full speed. It was well she could run so swiftly, for only a little way behind her there were three fierce dogs. Louder and louder the dogs barked as they chased her. The poor fawn was terribly frightened. Her heart beat very fast from fear. She ran into the dark woods among the trees, but the dogs were close on her track. She saw that they were gaining on her every moment.

3. Not far away she could hear a woodchopper's ax. The sound was near a log hut. The man heard the barking of the dogs, and, looking up, he saw the beautiful fawn running toward him. The next moment the dogs came in sight.

4. With a stout stick the man beat off the dogs. As soon as they were out of sight, he turned, and saw the fawn standing by the wood he had been chopping. Her dark eyes sparkled, and her neck was outstretched as if to make sure that her enemies were gone.

5. The fawn seemed to know that the man was her friend, and that but for him she would have been torn in pieces. She let him come up to her and pat her head. Then she watched him as he brought her a pail

of water. She took both water and food
from his hands, and was not at all afraid.

The fawn stayed with her friend the
rest of the day and was glad to be near
him. But the next morning she was gone.

6. Some one asked the man why he did
not shoot her.

"*What!*" said he, "shoot a poor dumb
animal that had run to me for help? *No!*
I would rather go without my dinner for
a *week* than have harmed that poor little
fawn, that had asked me to protect* her."

– *Youth's Instructor.*

The Boy and His Cap (104)

1. I know a boy whose eyes are bright,
And sharper than a cat's at night.
He never even has to squint
When looking at the finest print.

2. A thousand things he's sure to spy,—
Things that *escape* his *mother's* eye.
But though his bright eyes fairly snap,
He never, somehow, sees his cap.

3. I've seen him hunt it everywhere,
   On every table, every chair,
   And when his strength was wasted, quite,
   His mother saw it, plain in sight.

4. I wonder if some fellow here
   Can make this funny thing quite clear—
   Can tell me why a bright-eyed chap,
   Can never, never find his cap.
   —*Rebecca B. Foresman.*

My Shadow ⁽¹⁸⁸⁾

Who wrote this poem? What do you remember about him? What other poems that he wrote have you read? Which one do you like best?

Can you tell why a shadow is sometimes very tall, and sometimes very short? Can you tell why the little boy's shadow did not go with him early in the morning?

1. I have a little shadow
     That goes in and out with me,
   And what can be the use of him
     Is more than I can see.
   He is very, very like me
     From the heels up to the head;
   And I see him jump before me,
     When I jump into my bed.

2. The funniest thing about him
   Is the way he likes to grow—
   Not at all like proper children,
   Which is always very slow;
   For he sometimes shoots up taller
   Like an India-rubber ball,
   And he sometimes gets so little
   That there's none of him at all.
3. He doesn't have a notion
   Of how children ought to play,
   And can only make a fool of me
   In every sort of way.
   He stays so close beside me,
   He's a coward, you can see;
   I'd think shame to stick to nursie
   As that shadow sticks to me!
4. One morning, very early,
   Before the sun was up,
   I rose and found the shining dew
   On every buttercup;
   But my lazy little shadow,
   Like an arrant* sleepyhead,
   Had stayed at home behind me,
   And was fast asleep in bed.

—*Robert Louis Stevenson.*

In a Minute ^(o)

Choose either this story or the next one to read aloud in class. This story tells how a mother duck taught a little girl a good lesson. Find out what the lesson was. Did any animal ever teach *you* a lesson?

Find the starred words. Which of them do you know the meaning of?

Ethel was out on the long plank* wharf*
when the dinner bell rang.
She was throwing cracker crumbs
to the cunning little baby ducks.

"I'll go in a minute," she said to herself,
as she broke another cracker into tiny bits.
How hungry the baby ducks were!

What fun it was to feed them!
Ethel forgot all about her dinner
and the big dinner bell.

She had only one cracker left
when Bruno came running down to her.
The old mother duck saw him
as he came bouncing over the planks.

"*Quack!*" she called loudly.

And what do you think?
Every one of those baby ducklings
went into the water with a *splash!*

"*Quack!*" said the mother duck again,
and all the little duckies
swam hurriedly after her.
They hid among the rushes*
that grew by the edge of the pond.

"Why," exclaimed Ethel in surprise,
"they didn't wait to gobble another piece.
They minded their mother
the *very first minute* she called them!"

Ethel stood still for a second, thinking.
Then she gave the basket to Bruno
and ran quickly into the house.

"Late, as usual," said brother Hal,

as Ethel came into the dining room,
and took her seat at the table.
"It's twenty minutes instead of one
that you waited *this* time."

"But it's the *last* time I'll be late,"
said Ethel firmly, "because—because it *is*."

And Ethel kept her word.
She had learned her lesson well.
No one knew *how* she learned it
but the big white mother duck
that taught it to her.

—*Youth's Instructor (adapted)*

A Little Gentleman (o)

Find what there is in this lesson that really makes a gentleman. What did Joe think made a gentleman? A boy and girl may read this story together, the boy being Joe, and the girl grandma. If you read it as a dialogue, read only the words that are spoken by each person. Learn the meaning of the starred word.

Said little Joe, one day,
"I'm going to be a gentleman
when I'm big like papa."

"But papa was a gentleman
when he was *little* like *you*,"

said grandma, who was sewing near him.

"Did he dress in grandpa's coat and hat,
and walk with his walking stick,
as I do with papa's sometimes?" asked Joe.

"No; he wore pinafores*
and a little straw hat,"
said grandma, stitching away.

Joe looked at her steadily,
as if he could not understand.

"Are you trying to think
how he *looked*, dear?" grandma asked.
"I didn't mean *that*.
I meant he *acted* like a gentleman.
Once, when his little cousin Kittie
came to play with him, he went to his box
and brought out the very best toy he had,
and said, 'This is for you, Kittie,
because you are a *girl*.'
And I think that did more
to make him a gentleman,
than a coat, hat, and stick
would have done."

—*Selected.*

A Box of Pearls [S]

As you read this story silently, find out what this box of pearls is, what injures the pearls, what is good for them, and how to take care of them.

Have you ever seen a real pearl?* How much was it worth? Not all people can afford to buy pearls. Men, called divers,* fish for them in the bottom of the sea.

If some very rich lady should give you a box of twenty costly pearls, would you carelessly allow dirt to get in among them? What would you think of a child who would let something get on the pearls that would eat ugly holes in them?

God has given to each baby boy and baby girl twenty beautiful little pearls. He has set them carefully in a little red box, each one in its own place. And these pearls are more precious than any pearls that divers ever took out of the sea.

If you take good care of these twenty small pearls, God will change them one by one for thirty-two larger and more valuable pearls. These larger pearls are for you to keep the rest of your life. He will give you some of them when you are about six years old. By the time you are fourteen years old, you will have twenty-eight beautiful pearls. A few years later God will give you the other four.

Perhaps you have already guessed that these pearls are your teeth, and the little red box is your mouth. God has given us our teeth so that we may bite off small bits of food and grind them very fine before sending them down into the stomach. Hens and other birds do not have teeth, so they swallow their food without chewing it. Instead of stomachs, they have gizzards,* and the gizzard is made to grind their food. But children's *teeth* are to grind *their* food.

If you do not take proper care of your pearls, they will not last a lifetime, as they should. They will decay, and then the dentist may have to pull them out and throw them away.

There are two things that cause poor teeth. First, it may be you have not eaten the right kind of food to make good teeth. If you want your pearls to be white and shiny, and strong to do their work, give them plenty of milk, Graham and whole-wheat bread, green vegetables, and fruit. And give them plenty of real exercise, like chewing crusts of bread, zwieback,* parched corn, or apples. But never use them for cracking nuts. Then they will grow strong and healthy.

The second reason why teeth decay is that they are not kept clean. The teeth should be cleaned at least twice a day,—after breakfast and after supper. No tidy housekeeper would think of using dishes and knives and forks from meal to meal without washing them, would she? And no

tidy little boy or girl will think of using the knives and forks that grow in the mouth without very carefully cleaning them from meal to meal.

The teeth should be brushed not only backward and forward, but up and down, and round and round, inside and outside. Still, brushing the teeth does not always fully clean them. Bits of food often get fastened between the teeth where the brush cannot get them out. The best way to get these out is to push a strong thread down between the teeth. A soft  wooden or quill toothpick may be used. But never use a pin or anything that will scratch the tooth.

If bits of food are left between the teeth, the warmth and moisture in the mouth make the food begin to decay. This forms an acid that will eat right through the hard shell of the tooth, just as carbolic* acid would eat through the skin of your hand. Pretty soon the germs will make such a fuss in that little hole that you will feel them, for you will have a painful toothache.

No one who uses tobacco will have white teeth. In a little while they will turn brown, and no amount of brushing will take this dirty color off. Teeth do not look like pearls after they have been stained with tobacco.

Did you know that the habit of breathing through your mouth instead of your nose may make your teeth grow crooked? Crooked teeth are more often caused this way than any other. So, you see, if you are to have good, even teeth, you must keep the nostrils* clean and healthy.

Boys and girls, look after that valuable box of pearls that God has given you.

Comprehension Test. Write these ten things in two columns; in one, write those that harm your pearls; in another, those that are good for the pearls.
1. Chewing food well
2. Eating whole-wheat bread
3. Eating green vegetables and fruits
4. Brushing the teeth after meals
5. Picking food out of them with a pin
6. Using tobacco
7. Breathing through your mouth
8. Drinking good milk
9. Cracking nuts with the teeth
10. Chewing bread crusts or zwieback

Penn's Treaty With the Indians [S]

This is a story about the early history of the United States. As you read it, find out why the Indians loved Penn. How long does it take you to find out?

William Penn was a Quaker.* He belonged to a class of people called the Society of Friends. Even the king he called "Friend Charles" instead of "King Charles." William Penn lived in England about two hundred fifty years ago. King Charles owed William Penn's father some money. To pay the debt, he gave Penn some land in America.

Some people who had come from Europe were living on some of the land that King Charles gave to William Penn. But all the land in America really belonged to the Indians, for they were here long before any white people came from across the ocean.

Penn would do nothing but what was just and honest. Before he came from England to look at the land, he wrote a letter to the Indians. He told them he would not let any of his people harm them. He told them he would pay them for the land the king had given him. He also wrote to the white settlers. He told them they might keep the land on which they were living. He told them they might help to make the laws for his new colony.*

After this, William Penn sailed from England, and came to America. When he saw the beautiful trees that grew on his land he wanted to call the country "Syl-va'-nia," which means "woods." But King Charles said the land should be named after William Penn. So the country was called Penn's-Sylvania, or Pennsylvania.

The ship that brought Penn to Pennsylvania was named "The Welcome." And he was indeed welcome both by white people and by Indians. When he landed, he sent word to the Indians to meet him under a big elm tree by the river. Hundreds of Indians came with their wives and children. They all sat down on the ground in the form of a half moon. The Indian king, or chief, sat in the front row in the middle. The old and wise men sat at his right and left. The younger ones sat behind them. They talked among themselves for a while. They made up their minds what they would sell the land for.

Then a wise old Indian arose. All the other Indians sat quiet. Not one of them smiled or whispered. The wise Indian came to Penn and took him by the hand. He told Penn that his words were the words the king had told him to speak. He told him

This picture shows William Penn making his treaty of friendship with the Indians. See how interested the Indians look! Which is Penn? Point to the "Treaty Elm."

The wampum belt the Indians gave Penn

the price they wanted for the land. Penn paid for the land, and then the Indian sat down.

Penn had a large paper on which he had written all his promises to the Indians and all the things he wanted them to promise him. These promises were to make them friends. It was called a treaty.* He read the promises to the Indians. They were promises of love and kindness. The Indians promised to live in peace with Penn and his people as long as the sun should shine.

One old Indian stood up and told Penn's words to the others. He spoke one sentence at a time. After each sentence they all gave a loud shout. That was their way of saying "Amen." If any trouble should ever come, they said that six Indians and six white men should meet and settle it. That would be the end of the trouble.

After the treaty was agreed to, both Penn and the Indians signed it. The Indians could not write. They signed the treaty by giving Penn a belt made of shell beads called wampum.* The belt was made of white wampum. In the middle they made a picture with purple wampum. The picture was a white man and an Indian. They had hold of each other's hands.

Penn gave the written promises to the great chief. He told the chief to keep the paper always so that his children and their children would know about the treaty. Then he gave them many presents. The Indians loved Penn because he treated them as brothers. They called him "Brother Onas," because he wrote with a feather, or quill pen, and *onas* is the Indian word for feather.

Penn's treaty with the Indians kept peace and love in his country for many, many years. Ever after that, the old elm tree where the treaty was signed was called the "Treaty Elm." One time, during the Revolutionary* War, the English were in great need of firewood. But the British officer would not let the soldiers cut down the Treaty Elm. He placed a guard under it to save it. In 1810, it was blown down by the wind. The circles at its heart showed that it was nearly three hundred years old. Now a marble monument stands on the place where this noble elm grew.

Comprehension Test

1. How did William Penn get the land that is now called Pennsylvania?
2. How did it come to be named Pennsylvania?
3. What was the name of the ship in which Penn came to America?
4. What shows that William Penn was an honest, just man?
5. What treaty did Penn make with the Indians?
6. How did the Indians sign the treaty?
7. What did the Indians call Penn? Why?
8. What was the "Treaty Elm"?
9. How was the Treaty Elm once saved? What became of it at last?
10. Find Pennsylvania on the map. Find England.
11. Ask your "Dictionary Teacher" when the Revolutionary War was fought, and why.

Did Bob Think? (S5)

Find your fifth silent reading rate, and mark it on your rate graph.

Bob was an old horse on my great-grandfather's farm. He was a very clever* horse. But it is not so much for his cleverness as for one thoughtful thing he did that his name has been handed down to us who live so long after him and who never saw him.

Bob was very fond of children. The boys who lived near used to have many a pleasant game with Bob on sunny afternoons, when he was grazing in the fields.

Sometimes the boys chased Bob, and sometimes he chased them. It was a funny sight to see the old horse running after a troop of boys, uttering a peculiar whinny that plainly said, "Isn't this real fun, boys?"

One day Bob was coming slowly through the one long street of the village, dragging a loaded cart behind him. There, right in the middle of the street, a little child was sprawling in the dust. No one noticed it until Bob and the cart were close upon it.

Was the child to be trodden under the horse's feet, or crushed beneath the broad wheels of the cart? No; for just as the mother rushed out of the doorway with a shriek, Bob reached down, seized the child's clothing with his teeth, and laid the little one safely on the footpath. It was done tenderly, quietly, and it was over in a minute. Then the wise horse went on as if he had done nothing surprising.

Do you wonder that we keep Bob's memory green? And isn't his thoughtfulness a lesson for children whose excuse for carelessness that injures others is, "I didn't think"? *Bob thought,* and his thinking saved the child's life.

—*Selected.*

What to Be ^(o)

Find five good things in the girl that this lesson tells about, and three good things in the boy.

1. If I a little girl could be,
     Well, just like you,
   With lips as rosy, cheeks as fair,
   Such eyes of blue, and shining hair,
     What do you think I'd do?
   I'd wear so bright and sweet a smile,
   I'd be so loving all the while,
   I'd be so helpful with my hand,
   So quick and gentle to command,
     You soon would see
   That every one would turn to say:
   " 'Tis good to meet that child to-day."
   Yes, yes, my dear, that's what I'd do,
     If I were you.

2. Or if I chanced to be a boy,
   Like some I know,
   With crisp curls sparkling in the sun,
   And eyes all beaming bright with fun,—
   Ah, if I could be so!—
   I'd strive and strive, with all my might,
   To be so true, so brave, polite,
   That in me each one might behold
   A hero,* as in days of old.
   'Twould be a joy
   To hear one, looking at me, say:
   "My cheer and comfort all the day!"
   Yes, if I were a boy, I know
   I would be so.

   —*The Independent.*

Peter Paul Augustus [O]

Find out from these stanzas what Peter Paul Augustus decided to do. Do you think he made a good decision? Why?

1. Said Peter Paul Augustus:
   "When I am grown a man,
   I'll help my dearest mother
   The very best I can.

I'll wait upon her kindly;
  She'll lean upon my arm;
I'll lead her very gently,
  And keep her safe from harm.

"But when I think upon it,
  The time will be so long,"
Said Peter Paul Augustus,
  "Before I'm tall and strong,
I think it would be nicer
  To be her pride and joy
By helping her my very best
  While I'm a little boy."
              —*Author Unknown.*

Grandpapa's Spectacles [O]

As you read these stanzas, decide which of the children really loved grandpapa best. How do you know? Which was the most unselfish?

1. Grandpapa's spectacles cannot be found;
  He has searched all the rooms,
    high and low, round and round;
  Now he calls to the young ones,
    and what does he say?
  "Ten cents to the one who will find them to-day!"

2. Then Henry, and Nelly, and Edward, all ran,
   And a most thorough hunt for the glasses began;
   And dear little Nell, in her generous way,
   Said, "*I'll* look for them, grandpa,
         without *any* pay."

3. All through the big Bible she searches with care,
   That lies on the table by grandpapa's chair;
   They feel in his pockets, they peep in his hat,
   They pull out the sofa, they shake out the mat.

4. Then down on all fours, like good-natured bears,
   Go Harry and Ned under tables and chairs,
   Till, quite out of breath, Ned is heard to declare
   He believes that those glasses are *not anywhere*.

5. But Nelly, who, leaning on grandpapa's knee,
   Was thinking most earnestly where they *could be*,
   Looked suddenly up in the kind, faded eyes,
   And her own shining brown ones
         grew big with surprise.

6. She clapped both her hands—
         all her dimples came out—
   She turned to the boys
         with a bright, roguish* shout:
   "You may leave off your looking,
         both Harry and Ned,
   For there are the glasses *on grandpapa's head!*"

   —*Elizabeth Sill.*

Reading Tests and Scores for the Second Period

Boys and girls, you are now ready for your second period reading tests. When you have had these tests, your teacher will give you a grade in *silent* reading, in *oral* reading, and in *memory* reading. Before you take the tests, read again the lesson on page 79. How much have you improved since school began?

THIRD PERIOD

Reading Drills for the Third Period

Pronunciation Drills

1. During this period, you should learn the sounds and markings of *i*, *u*, and *y*.

Sounds of *i*
ī, as in īce
ĭ, as in ĭt
ï, (=ē), as in bïrd
ï, (=ē), as in machïne

Sounds of *u*
ū, as in ūse
ŭ, as in ŭs
u̞, as in pu̞t
ṳ, as in rṳle
û, (=ï, ē), as in fûr

Sounds of *y*
ȳ, (=ī), as in mȳ
y̆, (=ĭ), as in lovel y̆
ỹ, (=ī), as in mỹrrh

When you know all the markings and can use them, you will never need to ask anyone how to pronounce a single word. You can learn them all by yourself! Won't that be fine!

Other Drills

Keep on using your dictionary, too. Watch all the words that have a star after them, and always look them up in the dictionary.

Learn how to mark your stories into phrases. Make the phrases as long as you can read at one glance. Then practice reading them over and over. In this way you will learn to do your silent reading rapidly and your oral reading smoothly and easily.

Even the Winds Obey Him ^(S)

This story happened in Europe after the World War. Find Europe on the globe. When was the World War?

Read silently. Then tell how God answered the prayers of the family that this story tells about.

It was in Europe, just after the World War. The war was over, but there was still trouble in many places. A family who kept the Sabbath were living in a village that was surrounded by soldiers. The soldiers were placed where they could shoot anyone who tried to get out of the village. Then they set fire to the town.

The houses in that country have thatched* straw roofs. At this time, everything was very dry, and a strong wind was blowing. It was driving the flames straight toward this family's house. The whole town was rapidly being burned.

"Father, what shall we do?" the mother and the children asked. "We shall surely perish. Let us run!"

"If we run out, the soldiers will kill us,"

the father answered. "I believe God will keep us, for He has given me the promise, 'I shall not die, but live, and declare* the works of the Lord.'"

Then father, and mother, and children all knelt down and began to pray. As they prayed, the fire came closer and closer. At last, the house next to theirs began to burn. The fire came within two feet of their roof. But they kept on praying.

Suddenly, they heard a strange sound. They looked out to see what it was. They saw that the wind had changed, and was blowing right away from their house. It was blowing so strongly that the fire could not touch them. God had heard their prayers. They were saved.

"I know there is a God in heaven, and that He hears the prayers of His children," the father said. "We are never in danger when the Lord is with us."

Surely, even the winds obey Him.

Pretty Polly [O]

When you read this story orally, see how well you can imitate a parrot, especially the words Polly drawled out. What shows that Polly seemed to understand what the children said? What is there queer about a parrot's toes and bill? Do you know a good parrot story? Find Michigan on the globe or map.

There are a great many pretty pollies in the world. This one was owned by a lady in Michigan.* The lady lived in a house with high, stone steps, on one of the wide streets of a large city.

The cage for the parrot stood in the bay window. In the morning it was open for a while, and Polly hopped about outside.

All the little children on that street knew

and loved Polly. Some of them had to go past the house to go to school. They always looked to see if the window was open, or if Polly was out of her cage. If she was, she would hop down to the post to see them.

Then they would give her a bit of cake, or a cracker, or some other nice thing. Polly was sure to pay them with some of her wise looks or queer sayings.

If older people said, "Good morning, Mistress Polly," she would sometimes drawl out, "Good m-o-r-n-i-n-g. Polly's sleepy!"

To the next she might say, "Good morning. Don't bother a bird."

The children were sometimes late at

school, because they stopped too long to talk to her.

The one who saw the bird first called out, "Look, look! Polly is out of her cage!"

May was the one who could make her talk best. She went behind her and held out a bit of cake. "Here, Polly," she would say, "you know me."

"Y-e-s," drawled Polly, "I know you. You are good children."

That made them laugh, and Polly did not like that.

"Don't laugh," May would say.

When Polly had all she wanted, she would say, "Go to school now, children. Go to school!"

Then off they would run as fast as they could, for they knew it must be time.

This would all be said over again the next day, but each time it seemed just as funny as before.

Sometimes the children used to talk about her strong, stout legs.

"How her toes point,—two straight in

front, and two back!" they would say. Or, "What a queer bill she has, and how funny she looks when she eats!"

Polly did not seem to like to have them talk about her in this way.

"I don't blame her," said May; "we would not like to have anyone do it to us. We won't do it any more."

They hoped she would say some new thing. But she had only three sayings for them: "I like you," "You're good children," and "Go to school."

Polly had one bitter enemy, and that was Jim, the black cat.

Fly-Away (O)

Read this story, and find out what shows that Harry was generous. What gives anyone the best time? Find the place which shows that Harry answered his "alarm clock" at once.

Harry's birthday came in the winter. His aunt gave him a new sled for a birthday present. It was a real beauty. It was painted black,

with bright-colored flowers on it.
On the side in gilt* letters
was its name,—"Fly-Away."

The first good day for coasting,*
Harry went out to try his new sled.
He thought it had just the right name,
for it did "fly away" down the hill,
sure enough.

Pretty soon, he saw Fred Cole
looking at his present with wistful* eyes.

"Here, Fred," said Harry,
"don't you want to try my new sled?"

"Yes, indeed, if I may," said Fred.

"Well, then, jump on
and see how you like my 'Fly-Away.'"

"It's splendid,"
said Fred, with sparkling eyes,
as he came back up the hill.

After Fred had several coasts,
Harry took the sled again.
I think the reason he had such a good time
the rest of the day
was that he was so kind to Fred,
who had no sled of his own.
What do you think about it?

A Two-Thousand-Dollar Mouse House ^(S*)

Find your silent reading rate, and mark it on your rate graph.

Find out who built this mouse house, and why it cost so much. Why would this little mouse have found carpets useful to him? How long does it take you to find in your "Little Dictionary Teacher" the four starred words? Guess at their meaning first, then see if your guess is like the meaning given in the dictionary.

8
14
21
28
37
44

He was a clever little mouse that wished to go to housekeeping. But he lived in a house where there were no carpets, and the man who lived alone in the house was so careful that he never left the smallest thing about that

174

could be nibbled and made soft for a mouse's dainty house. So, where could mousie get material to build a nest?

Cold weather would soon come, and the wind did blow so hard through the cracks of the house! There was no place but the bare corner between the outer and inner walls of the old house where the little mouse could live.

One day mousie found a box! While the owner was gone, he nibbled a hole in it. In the box he found some pieces of paper. They would be fine for his nest! He pulled some of the paper out, and carried it to the warmest corner. He worked hard carrying the paper, and shredding* it until it looked soft as wool. On this paper were pictures. Whether this mouse liked pictures, or whether it was an accident that he did not make wool of them, no one will ever know. But he left the pictures whole.

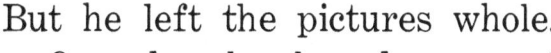

One day he heard a great deal of hammering near by. The

poor little mouse was so frightened that he scampered away. The hammering went on. At last, the men broke through into the very corner where the little mouse had built his comfortable nest. The moment they saw the nest, they stopped hammering. The poor mouse saw that his pretty nest, especially the pictures, caused the wildest excitement.

The little mouse had built his woolly house of money that the man who lived alone had saved! The pictures were all carefully smoothed out, and from them it was found that mousie's nest was worth two thousand dollars. How much more it cost, no one could tell but the miser* who owned the money, and he did not speak. The pictures were taken to the Treasury* Department at Washington, D. C.,* and redeemed;* that is, good money was given for them.

—*Youth's Instructor* (adapted)

The Ant and the Cricket ^(o)

As you read these stanzas, find out how they show the truth of Paul's words in 2 Thessalonians 3:10. How do they make you think of Proverbs 6:6-8? How long does it take you to find the starred words in your "Dictionary Teacher"?

---

1. A silly young cricket, accustomed* to sing
    Through the warm, sunny months
        of gay summer and spring,
    Began to complain when he found that at home
    His cupboard was empty and winter was come.
        Not a crumb could be found
        On the snow-covered ground;
        Not a flower could he see,
        Not a leaf on a tree:
    "Oh, what will become," says the cricket, "of me?"

2. At last, by starvation and famine* made bold,
    All dripping with wet and all trembling with cold,
    Away he set off to a miserly* ant,

        To see if, to keep him alive,
            he would grant
        Him shelter from rain,
        And a mouthful of grain.
        He wished only to borrow,
        He'd repay it to-morrow;
    If not, he must die of starvation and sorrow.

3. Says the ant to the cricket:
   "I'm your servant and friend,
   But we ants never borrow, we ants never lend.
   But tell me, dear sir, did you lay nothing by
       When the weather was warm?"
       said the cricket, "Not I.
       My heart was so light
       That I sang day and night,
       For all nature looked gay."
       "You sang, sir, you say?
   Go, then," said the ant, "and dance winter away."
   Thus ending, he hastily lifted the wicket,*
   And out of the door turned the poor little cricket.
   —*Frances Jenkins Olcott.*

Ratu Meli, a Native Chief of Fiji [S]

We all love Ratu Meli, and perhaps you have seen him. As you read this story, find as many reasons as you can why we love him. What changes did Jesus make in his life when he became a Christian?

Find his home on the globe or map. Trace on the globe his trip from Fiji to Milwaukee. Trace the journey of "The Pitcairn" from San Francisco to Fiji. This would be a good story to read aloud to some one.

Here is a picture of a native chief from Fiji.* His name is Ratu Meli.* His island home is far out in the Pacific Ocean. It is east of Australia.*

How do you like Ratu Meli's native dress made from the bark of a tree? In his hand is a war club.

A few years ago, Ratu Meli and his people, the Fijians, did not know the true God. They did not know about Jesus. They did not know about God's law and the Sabbath. They did not know about the new earth. They did not know that Jesus is soon coming back to this earth.

Then God's people gave money to build a missionary ship. This ship was named "The Pitcairn."* To help build it the children in the Sabbath schools gave their money. At last, the ship was built. It sailed from San Francisco to the islands of the Pacific Ocean. It sailed to Fiji.

The missionaries who sailed on the ship told the people of Fiji about Jesus. They told them that soon Jesus was coming from heaven to this earth. They told them of the beautiful home He is making for all who obey Him. They told them to get ready to go to their home in heaven.

Thirty years ago, Ratu Meli heard these strange and wonderful truths through a little paper and tract sent out from our small printing office in Fiji. He gave his heart to God. He stopped drinking Fijian grog, an intoxicating* drink made from the root of a shrub. He put away his great war club. He no longer followed the fashions by painting his face to make it blacker. He gave up his work as a government chief. He became a worker for God. For years he traveled and labored with our white missionary.

"I have never once seen Ratu Meli cross," said the missionary. "He never has the blues. He never complains when the sea is rough and his clothes are wet through.

Here is Ratu Meli at Milwaukee. Do you know the name of the white missionary with him?

Sometimes we are unable to cook our food. He just smiles and says, 'Let us endure this for the sake of the Master.' When the cook boy burns the food, Ratu Meli says, 'Bring it along. Let us eat it. It is good food.'"

The truth of God has made this wonderful change in his heart. It has made him always happy. It has made him overlook the faults in others, and to look on the bright side of everything. In 1926 he visited the United States. He went to the General Conference at Milwaukee.*

"Are you homesick, Ratu Meli?" some one asked.

"No," he answered. "I think of the cross of Christ every hour, and that keeps me from getting homesick."

"What about the food you have over here? Is it good?" some one else asked.

"I want to say that the food is very good in America," he answered. "But better than all the good physical* food you have given me is the spiritual* food I am getting right here in this Conference. Better than the best food this earth can give is the food Jesus will give us when we sit around that long silver table in heaven."

Ratu Meli has never worn shoes. To him they would be very uncomfortable. In Milwaukee, the wind from off Lake Michigan is sometimes very sharp and cold.

"What about your feet? Aren't they cold?" some one asked him.

"It is impossible that I should be cold in a place like this," he answered. "I am filled up with the warmth and blessing of God.

I had my shoes on last night when I came to the meeting, but I took them off. I got too hot. I couldn't stand it."

When Ratu Meli heard some of our Christian songs, he said: "Isn't that beautiful? That makes me think of a time when the Lord will come, and we shall all be gathered home and sing a song together."

This chief is very fond of children. Often, while in America, he was surrounded by a group of them, their happy faces looking into his kind eyes. They never tired of hearing him tell of his Christian life, and of his joy in the Lord.

"My joy it is impossible to tell," he said one day. "Nor can I show my thanksgiving. If I were a dog you would see my tail wagging with the greatness of my joy."

The Weather (101)

There are two word pictures in this poem. What do you see in each one? Which weather would be better for coasting? for a picnic? Which season of the year does each stanza describe?

1. Sometimes the weather is a man
     With gray cloak flying free;
   His coat of mail* is icy hail,
     A stormy steed* rides he.
   I cuddle in my bed at night
     With curtains gathered fast,
   While just outside the window pane,
   With clinking* spur* and rattling rein,*
     He gallops,* gallops past.

2. Sometimes the weather is a girl
     With eyes of bonny* blue;
   Gay flowers twined in every curl,
     Green buckles on each shoe;
   Her mantle's* wrought of shining gold,
     Her face is sweet with fun;
   She reaches out and takes my hand,
   And, laughing, through the happy land
     We run, *run*, RUN!

   —*Nancy Byrd Turner.*

My Chickadee Guests (S)

This story is about a man who loved birds. See how quickly you can read it and find out what birds ate at the table he prepared for them, what food he gave them, and how he got the chickadees to be guests* at his own table.

1. The air was cold, the snow was very deep, and many of the little wild birds were finding it hard to get their winter food. Some of them were dying because they could not find enough to eat. So I invited all the birds around my home to come and be my guests for the rest of the winter.

2. Just outside my study window I kept a tray filled with hemp,* millet,* sunflower seeds, cracked nuts, and lumps of suet.* There was another tray outside the bedroom window, and still another outside the window of the dining room. If snow fell and covered the food in the night, I brushed it off early the next morning.

Many hungry birds came there every day to feed. There were plump pine grosbeaks,* modest little redpolls,* and one saucy little

Match each picture with the paragraph in the story that tells about it.

siskin* that seemed to think he owned the whole garden.

Then there was a band of bluejays, that always acted as if they were stealing the food and were afraid of being caught at it. They did not stay to enjoy a quiet meal as the grosbeaks did, but grabbed all the food they could carry, and flew off with it. And there was an old hairy woodpecker that came for the suet. He spoke in a very loud voice, and acted as if he didn't want to be interrupted.

3. The friendliest of all were the chickadees. They always seemed as glad to see me as I was to see them. They would come in a little flock, and if I happened to be in the garden, they would alight upon my hands and shoulders, and almost ask me for something to eat.

4. One morning when I awoke, I heard a tapping at my window pane, and there I saw four little chickadees sitting in a row on the window sill, looking into the bedroom. Snow that had fallen in the night had covered all

the food in the trays, and it seemed as if the little birds were trying to make me hurry with breakfast.

5. I decided to invite them in to have breakfast with me. I dressed quickly, went downstairs, and pulled the breakfast table close to the window. On the tablecloth I sprinkled broken nuts, for chickadees are very fond of nuts. Then I opened the window and whistled. In a few moments the birds came down to the window ledge.*

For a moment or two they stood peeping into the room and looking at the food on the table. Then, one after another of the little birds flew in, and snatching up the bits of nuts, flew out into the garden to eat them.

Now this was very rude, for when you are invited to breakfast, you are supposed to eat at the table. So I thought I would give them a lesson in politeness. First of all, I swept up the little bits of broken nuts, and then with a needle and thread I stitched several large pieces to the tablecloth.

When the chickadees came back, they tried to pick up the nuts, but they could not do it. This seemed to make them angry, for they flew out of the window and sat in the bushes near by, scolding me.

6. But scolding did not make them less hungry, so back they came. By this time, I was eating my own breakfast—with an extra coat on, because the window was open. A chickadee alighted on the edge of the table and stood looking at me from under his little black cap. I sat very still, and he hopped over to half an English walnut. He tried to pick it up, but the thread held it fast.

Then he pecked at the kernel and looked up at me. I never moved, and he tried it again. He seemed to like the taste of the nut, so, holding on to the edge of the shell with his claws, he settled down and enjoyed himself.

The other chickadees looked in and saw him feeding there. One by one they followed him, until there were five birds eating breakfast with me. One of them came so near that his tail brushed my fingers. At first they were very nervous and would fly away if I moved my hands. But they always came back, and finding that there was nothing to be afraid of, they sat at the table, or on it, rather, until they had finished.

There have been many guests at my table since that day, but few have given me more pleasure, and certainly none have been more welcome, than those hungry little chickadees. —*Ernest Harold Baynes.*

Comprehension Test

1. In what season of the year was this story?
2. What did the birds find it hard to get?
3. Name three things that the man who wrote this story gave them.
4. Where did he put the food?
5. Name six kinds of birds that came to eat.
6. Which bird do you know, and how did he act?
7. Which birds were the most friendly?
8. How did they ask the man for their breakfast one morning?
9. Where did he at last put their breakfast?
10. What did he do to get them to come close to him?

Naomi (S2)

This story is for your second silent reading drill, or practice test, in the third period. It is about a little girl whose parents were cannibals. See how quickly you can read it and find out where she lived, why some of the people gave up being cannibals, and what happened because she was true to God.

Na-o′mi was an old black woman who lived in Fiji. When she was a little girl, all the people of Fiji were cannibals.* Cannibals are those who kill and eat human beings. Naomi's father and mother were cannibals.

Naomi had seen many dreadful things done in her own village. She had seen her own friends killed with great clubs, and taken away to be baked in a big oven and eaten by enemies. How terrible!

Years later, some of the people of Fiji became Christians. Then they stopped being cannibals.

Naomi had grown to womanhood. She heard that Jesus was soon coming to this earth. She believed that Jesus loved her. She believed that He was making a home in heaven for all who would obey Him. She decided to obey Him, for she wanted to be ready to meet Him when He should come.

Her own family were fond of eating pig's flesh. They were fond of smoking tobacco, and drinking intoxicating drinks. When Naomi heard the message of salvation, she decided that it was not right to use these unclean things, and she stopped using them. She decided to keep God's holy day, the Sabbath.

Her people were angry with her, and persecuted* her. They said she had no right to do these things unless they were willing. They said if she did not give up the truth, they would put her in jail.

But Naomi could not disobey God, not even to please her own people.

"I am willing to suffer anything for the truth," she said, "but I will not give it up."

One morning, they took her from her village. They took her to the native ruler, twenty-five miles away. The road was rough, the sun was hot, and Naomi was hungry and thirsty. They told the ruler that she would not obey their laws.

Naomi was brought before the judge. He asked her what she had done. She told him she had stopped eating pig's flesh, she had stopped smoking tobacco and drinking intoxicating drinks. She told him she wanted to obey the true God, and keep His holy Sabbath day.

The judge said she had done nothing that should cause them to put her in prison.

Then her people took her home again, over the same long, rough road, with no food to eat and no water to drink. They beat her with sticks, hoping that she would give up the truth she loved so well. They beat her so cruelly that even when she became an old woman, great scars were left on her body.

But with a smile on her face, she said, "I would rather die than give up the truth, because it means so much to me. When the Lord comes from heaven, I am sure He will take me to live with Him."

Week after week, for several years, her people persecuted her very cruelly. At last they knew that she would never go back to their ways. They watched her closely. They noticed that all the time she lived a godly life. Then they stopped persecuting her, and some of them became Christians.

Naomi now rests in her grave. Her last words were: "I have finished the course, I have run the race. There is laid up for me a crown of righteousness."

Many of her people now love and obey the truth. They feel very sorry for the way they persecuted faithful Naomi.

Comprehension Test

1. Where did Naomi live?
2. What wickedness did her parents practice?
3. When the people became Christians, what did they stop doing?
4. When Naomi became a Christian, how was she persecuted?
5. Why did her people at last stop persecuting her?

Don't Give Up [87]

Did you ever watch a baby bird try to fly? Did it give up and cry because it could not fly well at first? Did you ever see a tree bent far over in a windstorm? This poem tells the lesson you can learn from the birds and the trees. Find it.

How far along are you in your memory reading?

---

1. If you've tried and have not won,
    Never stop for crying;
   All that's great and good is done
    Just by patient trying.

2. Though young birds, in flying, fall,
    Still their wings grow stronger;
   And the next time they can keep
    Up a little longer.

3. Though the sturdy* oak has known
    Many a blast* that bowed her,
   She has risen again, and grown
    Loftier* and prouder.

4. If by *easy* work you beat,
    Who the more will prize you?
   Gaining victory* from defeat,*
    That's the test that *tries* you!

—*Phœbe Cary.*

To a Honeybee [82]

As you read this poem aloud, see how well you can hum as the bee hums.

1. Busybody, busybody,
   Always on the wing;
     Wait a bit
     Where you have lit,
   And tell me what you sing.

2. Up and in the air again,
   Flap, flap, flap!
     And now she stops,
     And now she drops,
   Into the rose's lap.

3. Come just a minute, come,
   From your rose so red;
     "Hum-m! Hum-m!
     Hum-m! Hum-m!"
   That was all she said.

4. Busybody, busybody,
   Always light and gay;
   It seems to *me*,
     For all *I* see,
   Your work is only *play*.

—*Alice Cary.*

Stories of Lincoln [O]

Read silently these two stories about Abraham Lincoln. Then choose one and study it until you can read it well to the rest of the class. Give each of the stories a name. When is Lincoln's birthday?

I. ─────────────

Abraham Lincoln
had a very strong love of fair play.
This was so well known
that he was often called upon

Lincoln

to settle disputes* among the neighbor boys.
In this way, he came to be looked upon
as the peacemaker of the village.

One day,
a quarrel arose between two boys
who were very much smaller than Lincoln.
Lincoln was called in.
He decided which of the boys was right.
The other boy became angry because
the dispute had been decided against him.

"See here, Abe! I'll lick you!"
he said boastfully* to Lincoln.

Lincoln was very tall. He looked down
at the small boy who dared him to fight.

14   Low Third

"All right, but let's fight fair,"
answered Lincoln. "You are so small
there isn't much of you for me to hit,
and I am so big
that you can't help hitting me.
So you make a chalk mark on me
that will show just your size,
or else you will have the advantage* of me.
When we fight,
you must hit me inside this mark,
or it will not count as fair."

The idea was so funny
that the boy began to laugh. Of course,
that took all the anger out of him.
And the quarrel ended as a joke.

II.

At another time,
Lincoln came upon a poor man
who was chopping an old hut into firewood.
The day was bitter cold,
and the man looked too weak
for such hard work.
He was barefooted and so thinly dressed
that he was shivering with cold.

"See here," Lincoln called out,
"how much do you get for this job?"
"One dollar," said the man.
"I must have the dollar to get some shoes."
"You go home and warm yourself,"
said Lincoln, taking the ax from him.
Then Lincoln swung the ax
as only Lincoln could,
and in a short time,
the old hut was chopped into firewood.
The poor woodchopper got his dollar
and his shoes, and he never forgot
the kindness of Abraham Lincoln.

—Adapted from "The True Story of Lincoln."

Washington's Love for Children ^(S)

One time, Washington was invited
to dine* with some friends.
The large house was brilliantly* lighted.
The table was beautifully decorated.*
It was spread
with fine silver and shining glassware.*
The good dinner was all ready.
The other guests* were there,
but where was General Washington?
Every one was waiting for him.
The dinner was spoiling,
and the host* wondered
why Washington did not come.
Then one of the servants
said that a guest had come an hour before,
and he had shown him to a room
so that he could wash and rest before dinner.
The host waited a little longer,
but still Washington did not come down.

Then he excused himself to his guests
and went upstairs.
On his way he passed the nursery.*

There sat the missing guest,
a baby astride his foot.
He was "riding the child to Boston,"
and singing as if he enjoyed the fun
as much as the baby did.
Another child stood close by
laughing with delight.

When Washington saw his host,
he was a little embarrassed,*
but he finished the song. Then he rose
and bade the children good night.

"Say, 'Good night, and thank you,
General George Washington!'"
said the father.

"Good night, and thank you,
General George Washington,"
the children called out after him.

How happy those children must have been
as they grew older, to remember the time
when Washington forgot his dinner
to play with them!

A Little Slave's Faith (S3)

1. A missionary in India,
passing one day through the schoolroom,
saw a little boy in prayer.

He heard him say,
"O Lord Jesus, I thank Thee
for sending a big ship into my country,
and wicked men to steal me
and bring me here,
that I might hear about Thee and love Thee.
And now, Lord Jesus,
I have one great favor to ask of Thee.
Please send men with another big ship,
and let them catch my father and mother,
and bring *them* to this country,
that they may hear the missionaries preach
and may love Thee."

2. A few days afterwards,
the missionary saw him on the seashore,
looking very closely as the ships came in.

"What are you looking at, Tom?"

"I am looking to see
if Jesus answers prayer."

Watching for the "big ship"

For two years,
he was to be seen day after day,
watching the arrival of every ship.
One day, the missionary saw him
dancing about with great joy.
 "Well, Tom, what gives you so much joy?"
 "Oh, Jesus answers prayer!
Jesus answers prayer!" he exclaimed.
"Father and mother came in that ship!"
 And this was really true.

The Churn That Was Never Through Churning (S)

Find out from reading this story what the churn was, and what lesson the story teaches you.

Once there was a little girl who had to churn every day and every day. This little girl was servant to a woman who made butter. This woman had a great deal to do to make a living, and she needed the butter the churn made every day to help her do it. It was an old-fashioned churn, where you had to work the dasher, or churn handle, up and down, up and down, up and down, until by and by the butter was made.

So this little girl would come to the churn every morning, ready and glad to do the churning. Her mistress* would fill the churn half full of cream, then she would put in the dasher, then she would

An Old-fashioned Churn

put on the cover, which had a hole in the middle for the dasher handle to go through. And then this little girl would go to churning, up and down, up and down, up and down. And the cream inside, with the dasher going up and down, up and down, up and down, would churn around, and churn around, and churn around, until the cream would be all broken up, and the butter would come.

Well, one day this little girl had been churning, up and down, up and down, up and down, until she thought it was almost time for the butter to come. And she was thinking, "Now pretty soon I shall be all through this churning, for the butter will have come. Then I will go and rest my tired arms, and sit down in my rocking-chair and rest my tired legs, and lean back and rest my tired back, and I will take my dolly and rock her to sleep."

Just as the little girl said this to herself, what should her mistress do but come and open the churn and put in another

panful of cream! And she said, "Little girl, you will have to start your churning all over, for I have found some more cream that I want made into butter. And so you must keep on churning."

The little girl was very tired, but she was a good little girl, and wanted to help her mistress. So she set to work again with the dasher, churning up and down, up and down, up and down, while the cream went round and round, and round and round, trying to make the butter.

After about another hour the little girl said to herself, "It must be almost done now." And she lifted the cover, and took a peep inside. And sure enough, there were little specks of butter on the inside of the cover and on the top of the cream.

"Now just a few more dashes, up and down, up and down, up and down," the little girl said, "and then I shall be through my churning. Then I will go and rest my tired arms, and sit down in the rocking-chair and rest my tired legs, and lean back and rest my tired back, and rock and sing to my dolly."

But just as she said this—what do you think? Why, her mistress came again, and opened the churn, and the little girl thought she was going to gather the butter. But instead of that, she took another pan of cream and dumped it into the churn. And she said, "Little girl, here is another pan of cream for you to churn. It looks so good and it tastes so good that I just can't help putting it into the churn to make more butter."

And do you know, that poor little girl was so tired, standing up so long, and pumping that dasher up and down, up and down, up and down, to make the butter come, that she just couldn't go on any longer, and she sat down and cried!

My! I don't wonder at it a bit, do you? If you were that little girl, how would you like to churn and churn, up and down, up and down, with a churn that could never quit churning because it had some more cream put into it every hour to make the butter? You wouldn't want to be servant girl to a mistress like that, would you?

Your mamma loves you, and she knows that while little girls should help, they cannot keep on working all the while, but need some time to rest and to play with their dolls, and to run outdoors and play in the sunshine. And your dolly's mamma (who is *you)* wouldn't do that way to her little dolly girl, would she? And any good woman or any good little girl who was a good mistress, never would think of treating her little servant girl like that; now would she?

Would you like to know that little girl's name? Well, listen, and I will tell you. That little girl's name is *Stomach.* Yes, ma'am! *Stomach!* And her mistress is any little girl who has a stomach. For you know when you eat your breakfast, it goes down into your stomach, and there it is churned around, and churned around, and churned around, all the while it is digesting.* And it takes several hours to digest and go on; and then Stomach can have a rest. And she needs a rest very much, for she can't keep on churning, and churning, and churning all the time. She needs some time to rest, and go and sit down in her rocking-chair and sing to her dolly!

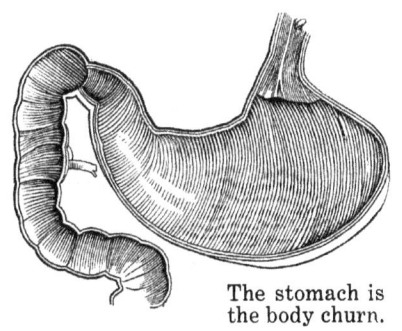

The stomach is the body churn.

But when any little girl mistress comes along after breakfast and dumps some more food down into her stomach, why, poor Stomach has to start all over again, and keep on churning and churning until the new food is digested. And then, if that little girl mistress should be so bad as to come and dump some more food in, why, I would not blame poor little Stomach if she just sits down and cries, would you? And let me tell you, if she gets to feeling so bad that she cries, her little girl mistress will be sure to know it, and *she* will cry, "Oh, oh! I have a stomach ache!"

So I think that the little girl mistress of the little servant Stomach should give Stomach just enough churning to do at breakfast, and never a bit more till noon, and then never a bit more till evening, and *never* eat between meals. And then good little Stomach will do her churning cheerfully and well every day, and everybody will be happy. That's what I think, don't you?

—*Arthur W. Spalding.*

Something to Do

Have you found the lesson this story teaches?

After you read the story, keep track of *your* little "servant" for one week, and report how many times you are unkind and unfair to it. Every time you do this servant a wrong, put a small pencil mark after the name of this story. It might be well for you to keep track for a longer time. I wonder how many boys and girls can go the rest of the year without putting down a single bad mark.

The Ill-Natured Brier ^(O)

Little Miss Brier* came out of the ground;
She put out her thorns,
  and scratched everything 'round.
"I'll just try," said she,
"How *bad* I can be;
At pricking and scratching,
  there's few can match *me*."

Little Miss Brier was handsome and bright,
Her leaves were dark green,
  and her flowers pure white;
But all who came nigh* her
Were so worried by her
They'd go out of their way
  to keep clear of the brier.

Little Miss Brier was looking one day
At her neighbor, Miss Violet, over the way;
  "I wonder," said she,
  "That no one pets *me*,
While all seem *so glad* little Violet to see."

Old Mr. Linnet,* who sat on a tree,
Heard the speech of Miss Brier,
  and thus answered he:

" 'Tis not that she's fair,
   For *you* may compare
In *beauty* with even Miss Violet there.

"But Violet is always so pleasant and kind,
So gentle in manner, so humble in mind,
   E'en the worms at her feet
   She would never illtreat,
And to bird, bee, and butterfly,
   always so sweet."

The gardener's wife
   then the pathway came down,
And the mischievous* brier
   caught hold of her gown.
  "Oh, dear, what a tear,
   My gown's spoiled, I declare,
That troublesome brier
   has no business there.
Here, John, dig it up;
   throw it into the fire."
And that was the end
   of ill-natured Miss Brier.

                —*Anna Bache.*

Little "Scotch Granite" (o)

This story is about a brave boy whom the other boys in school called "Scotch Granite." As you read, find out what shows that he was brave, why the boys named him "Scotch Granite," and what his real name was. This is a good story to learn to tell well.

Divide the first paragraph into phrases by short cross lines, and practice reading each phrase at a glance.

1. Little Burt and Johnny Lee were delighted when their Scotch* Cousin Willie came to live with them. He was as far along in his studies as they were, and the

first day he went to school they thought him a very good student. He wasted no time in play when he should have been studying, and he recited well.

2. At night, just before the close of school, the teacher called a roll,* and

213

the boys began to answer, "Ten." When Willie understood that he was to say "ten" if he had not whispered during the day, he replied, "I have whispered."

"More than once?" asked the teacher.

"Yes, sir," answered Willie.

"As many as ten times?"

"Maybe I have," he said slowly.

"Then I shall mark you 'zero,'" said the teacher sternly, "and that is a very great disgrace."

3. "Why, I did not see you whisper once," said Johnny that night after school.

"Well, I *did*," said Willie. "I saw others doing it, and so I asked to borrow a book; then I lent a slate pencil, and asked a boy for a knife, and did several such things. I supposed it was allowed."

"Oh, we *all* do *that*," said Burt, reddening. "There isn't any sense in the old rule, and nobody could keep it. Nobody does."

"I will, or else I will say I haven't," said Willie. "Do you suppose I would tell ten lies in one heap?"

"Oh, we don't call them *lies*," muttered Johnny. "There wouldn't be a credit among us at night if we were so strict."

"What of *that*, if you told the *truth?*" laughed Willie bravely.

4. In a short time, the boys all saw how it was with this truthful little Scotch boy. He studied hard, played with all his might in playtime, but from his own account he lost more credits* than any of the rest.

5. After some weeks, the other boys answered *nine* and *eight* oftener than they used to. Yet the schoolroom seemed to have grown much more quiet. Sometimes, when Willie Grant's mark was even lower than usual, the teacher would smile, but said no more of "disgrace."

6. Willie never preached at the boys or told tales. But somehow it made the boys ashamed of themselves, just seeing that this sturdy, blue-eyed Scotch boy must tell the truth. They felt like cheats and "storytellers." They talked about him among themselves and loved him, if they *did* nick-

name him "Scotch Granite,"* because he was so firm about a promise.

7. At the end of the term, Willie's name was very low down in the credit list. When it was read, he had hard work not to cry, for he *had tried hard* to be perfect.

8. The very last thing that day was a speech by the teacher.

"I want to give a little gold medal* to the most faithful boy, the one really the most conscientiously* perfect in his deportment,*" he said. "Who shall have it?"

"Little Scotch Granite!" shouted forty boys at once. For the child whose name was so low on the credit list had made truth noble in their eyes.

Is every boy in *your* school a "Scotch Granite"?

—*Sunday School Visitor.*

Bruno (S4)

This story is your fourth silent reading practice test for the third period. It is about a dog whose master lived in the Alps Mountains. Find on the globe or map where the Alps Mountains are.

Read and find out how this dog saved the life of his master and the little child at home.

A St. Bernard Dog

Bruno was a large St. Bernard* dog that belonged to a hunter who lived in a cottage among the Alps.

The upper parts of these mountains are very rocky and wild, and the paths are steep and dangerous. On the lower slopes are woods and green pastures, and in the valleys far below are beautiful little villages. In summer, the mountains are delightful. But in winter, the roads and paths are buried in snow, and travelers are often overtaken by storms, and perish in the bitter cold.

217

One winter night when the hunter came home, he found that his youngest child was very ill. There was no medicine in the house, and the nearest doctor lived in the village at the foot of the mountain. The child must have help as soon as possible.

The hunter called his dog, Bruno, and together they started down the mountain. The snow was falling fast, but they reached the village in safety. When the medicine was ready, the hunter and his dog went out again into the storm. The night was dark, and the snow had drifted over the road, so that it was very hard to find the way.

But with the help of his faithful dog the weary man struggled on until he was almost home. Then his strength began to fail, and he sank down into the snow. Bruno barked and rubbed his master's cheek, trying to make him rise and go forward.

"Yes, Bruno," said his master. "I will try once more." And he waded through the soft snow until he was within a few steps of his cottage door. The drifts grew deeper, and the hunter thought that he had lost his way.

"Bruno," he said, "I must lie down here and rest a little before I can go any farther."

Bruno knew that they were nearly home, and he was greatly troubled. He jumped about and barked, and tried in every way he knew to get his master to go on, but without success.

It is very dangerous to lie down to sleep in the cold and storm. People who do so seldom* wake again. They think that they wish to rest for only a few moments, and then they will be ready to proceed* on their journey. But it is the cold that causes the great desire to rest and sleep.

When Bruno found that he could not rouse his master, he turned his head toward the house and barked long and loud. The hunter's wife heard the barking, and knew the voice of the dog.

"My husband needs help," she cried, as she ran out of the cottage. Guided by the barking of the faithful animal, she soon found her way to the man who lay in the snow.

After much effort, she roused him from his sleep, and by her help he reached his home, with the medicine for his sick child safe in his pocket.

And thus it was that the hunter's dog, Bruno, saved the life, not only of his master, but also of the little babe that lay in the cradle. —*Jacob Abbott.*

Comprehension Test. Give the missing word in these sentences:

1. Bruno was a ——— dog.
2. He lived in the ——— Mountains.
3. In winter, the mountain roads are often buried in ———.
4. Bruno's master was a ———.
5. One stormy winter night, the master's youngest child was ———.
6. The master took ——— and went to the village for ———.
7. The village was at the ——— of the ———.
8. On his return, when he was nearly home, the master was ——— in the storm.
9. He was so ——— that he felt ———, and lay down in the snow to ———.
10. Bruno saved his master's life by ——— until ——— came to help him.

How the Street Sweeper Became a Minister [o]

This story is about a poor little orphan boy who swept the street crossings to earn money for a little food. As you read it, find out what happened one day that changed his whole life. See if you can find where he heard his "alarm clock." What shows that he was honest? truthful? industrious? courageous? studious? a Christian?

"A penny, ma'am?" asked a pale-faced, blue-eyed, thinly clad little boy of a lady as she was crossing one of the streets down town.

Taking out her purse, the lady gave the little street sweeper a five-cent piece, and passed on. In her haste she dropped her purse. The boy picked it up and was about to follow her and hand it to her. Just then he was surrounded by several other boys.

"How much is in it?" asked one.

"What will you do with it?" asked another.

"I am going to give it to the lady," was the boy's answer.

"Catch us so green as that!" shouted the others.

"No, no! come!" said the oldest boy. "We will have a good time."

"No, I *won't!*" said the little fellow, breaking away from them, and starting off in the direction the lady had gone.

He ran several blocks and made some mistakes. But at last he found the lady, and, taking off his cap, he gave her the purse.

The lady was surprised, for she had not discovered her loss. She asked him where he found it. The little boy told his story. The lady was at once interested in him.

"What is your name?" she asked. "And where do you live?"

"My name is Robert, and I live nowhere."

"Why, have you no father or mother?"

"No, ma'am. My father died when I was a baby, and my mother was buried some months ago." And passing his coat sleeve across his eyes, he wiped away the tears that were beginning to flow.

"And what do you do for a living?"

"I sweep the street crossings, and do what little I can to buy bread. Then at night I sleep in some wagon or on some step."

"Are you not afraid, Robert?"

"Sometimes. But mother told me before she died that if I would pray to God and read this Book, God would send some one to care for me."

As he spoke, he took a well-worn Testament from the inside pocket of his jacket.

This was enough for the kind-hearted woman. A short time before, she had lost a boy,—her only boy,—just about the age of the little street sweeper. She followed Robert into one of the back streets, where he said his mother had lived. She found he had told the truth.

Then she took the little fellow to her own beautiful home. She sent him to school, and cared for him as if he were her own child. When she found that he desired to be a preacher, she sent him to college. A few years ago he finished college, and now he is preaching the gospel.

Little children, do you think Robert was ever sorry that he returned the purse? Do you think he was sorry that he read the Bible and prayed to God every day?

—Selected.

Rosa Bonheur ^(S)

Something in this story makes me think of the new earth. Can you find out what it is? Would you like to have known Rosa Bonheur? Why?

Divide the first two paragraphs into phrases by short cross lines, and practice reading each phrase at a glance.

Rosa Bonheur and one of her friends

Rosa Bonheur lived in France, in the country. She and her brothers loved the woods and the fields. They loved to watch the shy* rabbits and the frisky squirrels. Sometimes Rosa would take her lunch and drawing paper and spend a whole day outdoors. She would make friends with any animal she could find. When she went home at night, she would take with her a picture of a squirrel, or a rabbit, or a dog.

Sometimes her pictures were not very good. Then her father could not help laughing at them. But she loved to draw, so her father told her to keep on trying. After a while, he let her come into his studio* and draw. Then she tried harder than ever. At last, even when she was just a little girl, she drew animal pictures that looked quite natural.

When Rosa was about ten years old, her father moved to the great city of Paris. They lived up several flights of stairs. Rosa missed the country with her animal friends. Just across the street was a butcher's shop. In front of the shop the butcher had a sign. It was a wild pig cut out of wood. Every time Rosa went by this shop, she would stop and pet the wooden pig.

While they lived in Paris, the children had a few pets. They had a parrot, a monkey, two dogs, some rabbits and birds, and a pet lamb. Their windows opened on the flat roof of a house. Here they made a garden and kept their pets. Every day Rosa's brothers carried the lamb down on their shoulders to a green field near by. Here it would nibble the grass, and have a run with the children. Then they carried it back to the roof. You will find this lamb in many of Rosa's pictures.

Rosa's mother died while they were living in Paris. Then Rosa went to the country to live with an aunt. She was glad to be in the country again. Sometimes on her way to school she would make a smooth place in the road and then draw wonderful pictures in the dust with a stick. She had such a good time drawing in the road that she often forgot to go to school, or was very late.

Rosa was very lonely without her father. She begged so hard to go back to him and paint pictures in his studio that he finally let her come. He was her teacher, and she was very happy. If she could only find an animal to draw, she was willing to walk

These pictures were drawn by Rosa Bonheur. The one at the top she named "Lions at Home." The other is "Shepherd and His Flock." Which of these do you like the better? Point to Nero.

miles in any kind of weather. She was even willing to go without food.

The first picture she painted that was shown with the pictures of other great artists* was some little rabbits nibbling carrots. People began to buy her pictures. Now she could help her father earn money.

After a while, she bought a farm in France. She put many wild animals on the farm. People sent her gifts of fine horses and other animals to paint. "Buffalo Bill"* once sent her two fine horses from Texas. Her pictures were now famous all over the world.

One of Rosa Bonheur's pets was a large lion, named Nero. Nero often lay near her as she worked on her paintings. Once, when she was leaving for a long trip, she had to send Nero away. When she came back, she found her pet in one of the parks in Paris. He was in a cage, sick and blind.

"Nero, my poor Nero!" she exclaimed, "what has happened to you?"

As soon as she spoke, Nero knew her

voice. He crept up to the bars of the cage, where she could pet him. Then Rosa Bonheur took him to her home, and cared for him as long as he lived. He died with his great head resting in her lap. She painted Nero in her pictures, "An Old Monarch"* and "Lions at Home."

When the French people wish to honor an artist, they give him the medal of the "Legion* of Honor." This is a white cross. One day, the empress* of France came to Rosa Bonheur's studio. It was a great event to have the empress visit anyone. They had a delightful visit. When she left, she hung the white cross around Rosa Bonheur's neck. No woman had ever before worn this medal.

Comprehension Test

1. On the globe or map, find where Rosa Bonheur lived. Which direction is it from your home? Point toward it.

2. Of what did she make drawings?

3. What were some of her pets when she lived in the city of Paris?

4. Which did she like best, the city or the country? Why?

5. What was her first great painting?
6. Name some of her other paintings that you have seen. Which do you like best?
7. What did "Buffalo Bill" do for her?
8. What shows that she loved animals?
9. How did the empress of France honor her?
10. Rosa Bonheur was born in 1822. She died in 1899. How old was she then?

Little Foxes (135)

This lesson tells about "the little foxes, that spoil the vines." How many little foxes are named? What are their names? What is the name of the "hunter" that catches each of these little foxes? Do any of these little foxes get among *your* vines? Be sure you get the right hunter after them, or you will have no rich harvest.

The boys might read in concert the lines that name the foxes, and the girls those that name the hunters. Then change about. Make it interesting by giving the right tone to the name of each fox. And remember, a good hunter never lags over his prey.

Among my tender vines I spy
A little fox* named—*By and By.*
Then set upon him quick, I say,
The swift young hunter—*Right Away!*

Around each tender vine I plant
I find the little fox—*I Can't.*
Then, fast as ever hunter ran,
Chase him with bold and brave—*I Can!*

No Use in Trying—lags and whines
This fox among my tender vines.
Then drive him low, and drive him high,
With this good hunter, named—*I'll Try!*

Among the vines in my small lot
Creeps in the young fox—*I Forgot.*
Then hunt him out and to his pen
With—*I Will Not Forget Again!*

A little fox is hidden there
Among my vines, named—*I Don't Care.*
Then let *I'm Sorry!*—hunter true—
Chase him afar from vines and you.

—Sunshine and Shadow.

What the Minutes Say [113]

1. We are but minutes; little things,
Each one furnished with sixty wings,
With which we fly on our unseen track,
And not a minute ever comes back.

2. We are but minutes; each one bears
A little burden of joys and cares;
Take patiently the minutes of pain,
The worst of minutes cannot remain.*

3. We are but minutes; when we bring
A few of the drops from pleasure's spring,
Taste their sweetness while yet you may,
It takes but a minute to fly away.

4. We are but minutes; use us well,
For how we're used you must one day tell.
Who uses minutes has hours to use;
Who loses minutes whole years must lose.

—*Author Unknown.*

Comprehension Test

1. What are the "sixty wings" of a minute? Would it have been just as well to say, "Each one furnished with sixty *feet?*" Why?

2. What will help us to be patient when in pain? Read the answer in stanza two.

3. When will the "one day" of the last stanza come?

"Soft-eyed reindeer crop the short grass in Eskimo land."

The Snow Baby (S5)

This story is your last silent reading practice test for this semester. How much have you gained since school began? The story tells about the Es′ki-mos and their home. Eskimos are Indians who live in A-las′ka and other places in the northern part of North America. Find Alaska on the globe or the map. In what direction is it from your home?

As you read this story, find the funniest thing in it. Notice what each of its four parts is about, and try to give each a name.

I. ―――――――――――

Hundreds and hundreds of miles away in the white frozen north, there is a wonderful land of snow and ice. There, strange little yellow people, called Eskimos,* live in houses of snow and dress in skins of animals.

In summer, in this wonderful land, the sun never sets. It shines all the time, day and night. Flowers spring up, and soft-eyed reindeer* wander about, cropping the short grass.

The ice breaks up and drifts out to sea. Great rivers of ice push forward into the water. Great mountains of ice, called icebergs, break off from them and float away like white ships.

An Iceberg

The blue waves dance and sparkle in the sun. Singing brooks rush down the mountains. Thousands of noisy sea birds come to the rocky peaks to lay their eggs.

Glossy seals* swim in the water, and once in a while a shaggy* white bear goes running over the floating ice in search of seals. The Eskimos, paddling swiftly through the water in their strange skin boats, hunt these animals for food and clothing.

In winter, there is no sunshine at all in Eskimo land. For four long, long months it is dark all the time, just as it is here in the night. The ground is covered deep with snow, and the poor deer must dig through it with their hoofs for grass and moss. The sea is covered with thick ice, and the birds fly away. The cold is so terrible that the Eskimos would freeze to death were it not for their thick, warm fur coats.

Seals

II. _____

Here, in this wonderful land there was found, one September day, a snow-white baby with big blue eyes.

And such a funny little house it was where she was found. It was only one story high. The walls were more than a foot thick, and the outside was covered with heavy black paper. All around the house was a veranda.* Its walls were built of boxes of biscuit, sugar, and other foods.

Inside the house, the little room where the baby lived was lined with soft, warm blankets. There was a bright carpet on the floor and pictures on the walls.

All these things, like the boxes of food outside, came in the ship that brought the baby's father and mother to this strange country.

One window of the baby's room looked out upon a great river of ice. From the other window you could see high red and brown mountains. And here was the sea in which strange-looking icebergs* floated.

III.

When the people of that land heard that there was a white baby in the small black house, they came hundreds of miles to see the little stranger.

They talked to the baby in their own queer language. They called her the Snow

Baby, and they brought her presents of fur mittens and little sealskin boots.

After the sun went away, the baby lived for days and weeks in a little room lined with blankets. A lamp was kept burning in the room all the time, both day and night.

One of the Eskimo women made a little suit of clothes for the baby, all out of furs. There were only two pieces in this suit. First, there was a pair of little trousers and boots made together. Over this was worn a coat with a warm hood.

IV. ———————

When summer came and the sun returned, the Snow Baby was taken out of doors every day. No matter how cold it was she had a sleigh ride on her little Eskimo sled. You should have seen her team of dogs with their bright eyes, their sharp-pointed ears, and their big bushy tails.

For nearly a year, the Snow Baby lived in this strange, northern home. But one day in August, a big black ship came up the bay. It was the same ship that had brought the Snow Baby's father and mother to the Snowland.

Then the baby and her mother went on board the ship, and steamed away south to their own American home.

—*From "The Snow Baby."*

Comprehension Test

1. Which of the four parts of this story might be named—"Eskimo Land"?
"The Baby's First Presents"?
"Leaving Snowland"?
"The Snow Baby's First Home"?

2. There are five races of people on the earth—the white race, the black race, the yellow race, the brown race, and the red race. To which race do the Eskimos belong?

3. What is strange about summer in Eskimo land?

4. What is strange about winter?

5. What two animals furnish the Eskimos most of their food and clothing?

6. With what was the Snow Baby's home lined?

7. What was the Snow Baby's carriage?

Mother's Boy [O]

The boys may read this poem to the girls.
What temptations did "mother's boy" have to meet? Why did he have a happy time at his play?

---

1. The snow was deep and heavy,
     And the laddie's hands were small;
  The shovel was too large for him,
     The handle very tall;
  But mother dear was washing,
     And with all his might and mind,
  A pathway to the clothes reel*
     He right bravely tried to find.

2. Though both his hands had blisters,
     And his arms were tired, too,
  And mother said, "Why, Billy,
     Let *me* finish that for you,"
  Though Tommy Jones was shouting,
     "Oh, you Bill! come out and play,
  And help me build a snow man
     In the field across the way,"

3. He labored with his shovel,
    Till at last his task was done;
  Then with a merry whistle,
    Off he ran to have his fun.
  Now let me tell you, boys and girls,
    He had a joyous day,
  Because he worked for mother dear
    Before he went to play.
               —*The Sabbath Recorder.*

Mother's Girl ^(O)

The girls may read this poem to the boys in the class. Count the things "mother's girl" did to help. Name them. Why was she a blessing?

1. Sleeves to the dimpled elbow,
    Fun in the sweet blue eyes,
  To and fro upon errands*
    The little maiden flies.

Now she is washing dishes,
   Now she is feeding the chicks,
Now she is playing with Pussy,
   Or teaching Rover tricks.

2. Wrapped in a big white apron,
   Pinned in a checkered* shawl,
Hanging clothes in the garden,—
   Oh, were she only tall!
Hushing the fretful baby,
   Coaxing his hair to curl;
Stepping around so briskly,
   Because she is mother's girl.

3. Hunting for eggs in the haymow,*
   Petting old Brindle's calf,
Riding Don to the pasture
   With many a ringing laugh.
Coming whene'er you call her,
   Running wherever sent—
Mother's girl is a blessing,
   And mother is well content.*

      —*Author Unknown.*

Reading Tests and Scores for the Third Period

You have now reached the middle of the school year. Are you halfway toward your goal in silent reading? The test that you are now ready for will show. You will take this test in just the same way as you took your tests at the end of the first and second periods.

Remember that it is better to get 100 in comprehension even if your rate is not quite so high as it should be, than to score a high speed and fail in comprehension. So when you read your silent test, *read thoughtfully*.

For your oral test, choose any story you like from the third period. Study and practice it as much as you please. Then remember to make your voice sound right, speak all your words correctly and very plainly, read only the words that are in the story, and look often away from your book without losing your place. Read slowly and smoothly.

You can give *yourself* a grade in memory reading by finding out how many words there are in all the poems you have learned this period. I wonder how many of you will have a grade of 100. This will be your grade if your memorized poems for the period total at least 300 words.

Your memory test will show how well you have remembered the important things in the stories you have read during this period.

The Little Dictionary Teacher

A

a-bŏm-i-nā′tion, something greatly hated.

ac-cŭs′tomed, used to; often done.

a-crŏs′tic, first letters of several lines which taken in order spell a word or phrase.

ad-van′tage, that which helps one to get the better of another.

af-fĕc′tion-ate, loving.

ăl′**pha**-bet, all the letters in their order.

ăm′bu-lance, a wagon or auto for carrying a sick or wounded person.

a-n**oi**nt′est, to pour oil upon as a religious act; to set apart for sacred use.

anx′ious-ly, being troubled.

ap-pēar′, come in sight.

ăr′rant, shameless; not ashamed.

ar-rīv′al, coming to a place.

är′tist, one who draws or paints beautiful pictures.

Aus-trāl′ia (ya), name of the smallest continent.

au̇′thor, one who writes a book.

B

băl′ance, pair of scales for weighing things.

băn′tam, a small kind of chicken.

blȧst, a sudden gust of wind.

blūe jay, a common bird that is looked upon as a thief.

bōast′ful-ly, in a proud, bragging way.

bŏn′ny, pretty.

brī′er, prickly rosebush.

brĭl′liant-ly, very brightly.

brŏŏk′let, a small brook or stream of water.

Bŭf′fa-lo Bill, a name given to a man because he once killed many buffaloes.

bū′reau (rō), a piece of furniture with drawers.

bûr′rōw, to dig a hiding place in the earth.

C

căn′ni-bals, savages who kill people and eat their flesh.

car-bŏl′ic, an acid used for killing germs. It is made from coal tar.

cär′pen-ter, a man who builds houses.

càsk′et, a coffin.

çĕn′tu-ry, one hundred years.

chĕck′ered, a pattern marked off in small squares.

chĭck′a-dee, a sociable little bird with a black cap.

clĕv′er, having great skill, or wisdom.

clĕv′er-ness, skill.

clĭnk-ing, rattling.

cōạst′ing, sliding down hill.

coat-of-māil′, a soldier's dress made of small pieces of metal joined together.

cŏl′o-ny, settlement.

com-plāin′, find fault.

com-plāin′ing, finding fault.

com-pre-hĕn′sion, understanding.

cŏn′fer-ence, a body of people met to discuss important matters.

con-s¢i-ĕn′tious-ly, in a way that one thinks is right.

con-sĭd′er, think about carefully.

con-tĕnt′, satisfied.

cor-rĕct′ly, without making a mistake.

cøûr-ā′ġøøus, brave.

crĕd′its, honor marks for good behavior.

crew, the sailors who belong to one boat.

crĭp′ple, one who has lost an arm, or is disabled in some other way.

cûr′rent, water flowing strongly in one direction.

D

D. C., District of Columbia, where Washington, the capital of the United States, is located.

de-clâre′, tell about.

dĕc′o-rat-ed, trimmed or ornamented with something beautiful.

de-fēạt′ conquer; beat.

de-pōrt′ment, behavior.

de-spâir, discouragement.

de-tọur′ing, going a long way around in order to get away from something.

dī′a-mond, a costly stone.

dic′tion-a-ry, a word book that tells the meanings of words.

di-ġĕst′ing, making food ready for use in the body.

dīne, eat dinner.

dis-cóv′ered, found for the first time.

dis-putes′, quarrels.

dis-tĭnct′ly, very plainly.
dī′vērs̱, men who dive into the sea for pearls and other things.
down′y, like fine, soft feathers, called down.
dwĕll, live.

E

ēa̸′ḡer, earnest.
ĕch′o, a sound that has bounded back.
em-băr′rass*e*d, shy and bashful; confused.
em-brāçe′, hug.
ĕm′press, a woman who rules a country as a queen does.
en-dūre′, put up with.
ĕr′rand, something to be done by some one sent for that purpose.
Ĕs′ki-mōs, a tribe of people living in the Far North.

F

făm′ĭne, a time when there is little or no food.
fa̤ẘn, a young deer.
Fï-jï, an island in the Pacific Ocean.
flăt′ter-ing, saying words that please one's pride.
flăt′ter-y, false praise.
flăx′en, of golden color.

flē*e*ç*e*, a sheep's wool.
fōld, a place where sheep are protected. To "fold" the sheep is to put them in the fold.
fōre′h̸ĕa̸d, that part of the face between the eyes and the hair.
fŏr′est, heavy woods.
fŏx, a sly, wild animal related to the dog.
frĭsk*e*d, played about.

G

găl′lops, runs in leaps.
Gĕn′ō-a, a town in Italy where it is supposed Columbus was born. The place of his birth is not certainly known.
ḡĭlt, covered with yellow like gold.
gĭz′zãrd, the part of a bird that grinds its food.
glá́ss′ware, dishes made of glass.
ḡlēa̸ms̱, shines.
ḡrăn′ïte, a very hard kind of stone.
grīnd′stone, a flat, round stone for sharpening tools.
ḡrŏḡ, a kind of drink that makes people drunk.
grōs′beak, a bird with a short, thick beak.

245

gu̵ĕst, one who is entertained at another's home; a visitor.

gŭt′ter, a ditch for carrying away water and dirt.

H

hâre, an animal like a rabbit.

hās′ten-ing, hurrying.

hāy′mow, a place where hay is stored, usually upstairs in a barn.

hĕa̵v′i-ness, great sorrow.

hĕmp, a plant that bears seed called hemp. Some kinds of coarse linen are made from this plant.

hē′rō, a man who has done a very brave act.

hŏs′pĭ-tal, a house where sick people are cared for.

hōst, one who entertains guests.

how′däh, a seat for riding on an elephant or a camel.

hŭt, a small, poorly built house.

hy̆mn̸, a religious song.

I

īce′berg, a mountain of ice floating in the sea.

in-dŭs′tri-ø̸us, very busy; not idle.

ĭn′flu-ence, power.

in-tĕl′li-gent, able to think well and understand; wise.

in-tŏx′i-cāt-ing, making drunk.

in-tro-dūç′ing, making known.

īs̸′land, a body of land with water all around it.

ī′vo-ry, the hard, bony, white material of the tusks of elephants.

J

jĕt, a shiny piece of deep black coal.

jŭṉ′gle, a dense thicket of trees and vines.

K

kĕn′nel, a house for a dog.

L

làss, a girl.

lĕd̸ġe, a shelflike edge.

lē′ġion, a large number.

lē′ī, a piece of money used in Roumania, which used to be worth about 20 cents. Since the World War, one lei has been worth about one half of one cent.

lĭn′ġered, waited about.

lĭn′net, a small bird.

lŏf′ti-er, very high; proud.

lŭl′la-bȳ, a cradle song.

M

mail, see coat of mail.

Măn'i-tou, the Indians' name for the Creator

măn'tle, a loose cloak.

mā'son, one who works with stone and plaster.

mĕad'ōw, a grassy field.

mĕd'al, a piece of metal appropriately stamped, used as a reward.

mĕm'o-rīze, learn by heart.

mēr'çў, kindness and forgiveness.

mĕr'ry, happy.

Mĭch'i-gan (sh), a state in the northern part of the United States.

mĭl'let, a kind of grain.

Mil-wau'kee, a city on Lake Michigan.

mĭs'chie-vøus, full of mischief.

mī'ṣer, one who piles up money instead of using it to help himself and others.

mī'ṣer-ly, like a miser.

mĭs'sion, a place where the gospel is preached to those who do not know Christ.

mĭs'tress, a woman who has charge of a home or a school.

mōld, leaf mold, soil made of decayed leaves.

mŏn'areh, a leading ruler. The lion is called the king of beasts, and therefore may be called a monarch.

mŏn'u-mĕnt, something built to keep a great person or event in memory.

mŏth'er-less, without a mother.

moun'tạin, a high hill.

Mt. Ro-rạī'ma, a mountain in South America where we have a mission. The "Davis" Indians live here.

N

nă'tion-al, having to do with one's country.

nā'tive, a person who is born in that country.

New'found-land dog, a large, shaggy-haired, black dog.

nigh, near.

Niñ'a (Neen'ya), the name of one of Columbus' ships.

nŏs'trils, passages through the nose.

nō'tion, an idea; what one thinks about something.

nûrse, or nursie, a woman who takes care of children.

247

nûr′ser-y, a room where children are taken care of.

O

oblīġ′ing, doing a favor with pleasure.

oc-cā′sion-al-ly, once in a while.

ōcean, the largest body of water.

ō′nas, Indian word for feather.

ōpe, open.

ō′ral, the spoken word.

ō′ral-ly, speaking for others to hear.

P

pälm′ tree, a tree that grows in warm climates.

Păn′sy, the childhood pet name of Mrs. Isabella Macdonald Alden, who wrote many books for children. She died in 1930 at her home in Palo Alto, California, at the age of 89 years.

pa-pōose′, an Indian baby.

pa-ren′the-sis ( ), marks that are sometimes used in writing or printing.

pás′tures, a grassy field where sheep and cattle feed.

pĕarl, a hard, smooth, white ball formed in the shell of a pearl oyster.

pĕas′ants, persons who live and work in the country.

pĕr′ished, died.

pēr′se-cūt-ed, illtreated for religious belief.

per-se-cū′tion, being persecuted.

per-se-vēr′ing, not easily giving up a task.

pĕt′als, the bright-colored leaves of a flower.

pe-tī′tion, prayer.

phy̆s′i-cal, for the body.

pĭn′a-fore, a child's loose apron.

pine grōs′beak, a bird with a stout beak.

Pĭn′ta, the name of one of Columbus' ships.

Pit′cairn, an island in the Pacific Ocean; our first missionary ship.

plănk, a thick board.

plŭck′y, having pluck, or courage.

pounçe, to spring upon quickly.

prep-a-rā′tion day, the day to prepare for the Sabbath.

pre-pâr′est, get ready.
prĕṣ′ĕnce, before others.
pro-çeed′, go forward.
prŏmpt, on time; without waiting.
pro-tĕct′, keep from harm.
prŏv′erb, a short, wise saying.
p̸sȧlm, a sacred song or poem written by David.

Q
Quāk′er, a person belonging to a religious class of people who dress very plainly and who say *thee* and *thou* instead of *you*.

R
Rä′tu Me̱′lĭ, a Christian chief who lives in Fiji.
reel, a clothes line so put up that it can be turned around in a circle.
re-deemed′, exchanged for good money.
rĕd′pōll, a bird with a red crown.
re̱in, a strap for holding a horse or other animal in check.
re̱in′deer, a large deer used in cold countries to carry heavy loads.
re-māin′, stay.

re-pēa̸t′, say over.
re-pēa̸t′ed, said over.
re-plȳ′, answer.
re-stōr′eth, bring back to its usual strength; to heal or make new.
Rev-o-lū′tion-a-ry War, the war that the United States fought against England for freedom. It was fought in the days of George Washington, more than 150 years ago.
re-wa̱rd′, a gift.
rig̸ht′eous-ness, right doing.
rōgu̸′ish, full of mischief or fun.
rŭsh′es, grasslike plants growing in marshy ground.
rōll, a list of people's names.

S
Sä′hib, a native word in India meaning *sir* or *mister*.
Sän′ta Ma-rï′a, the name of one of Columbus' ships.
Scŏtch, a person born in Scotland.
sēa̸ls, sea animals.
sēa̸′weed, weeds or plants that grow in the sea.

sĕl′dom, not often.
sēr′pent, a snakelike animal.
shăg′gy, with rough hair.
shĕp′herd, one who takes care of sheep.
shrĕd′ding, tearing into small strips.
shĭrk, sneak away from.
shȳ, bashful, timid.
sī′lent reading, reading to one's self.
sĭs′kin, a small, greenish-colored bird.
slŭḡ′ḡard, a lazy person.
slŭm′ber, sleep.
slŭm′ber-ing, sleeping.
sŏl′emn̸-ly, very soberly.
spĭn′ner, one who spins thread.
spĭr′it-u-al, for the soul.
spûr, an iron pin on a horseman's heel with which he pricks the horse to make it go faster; to hasten action.
spȳ, get sight of.
spȳ′glass, a small telescope for seeing objects far away.
squĭnt, look at without seeing in a true way.
stăḡ′ḡer, begin to fall.

stĕa̸d′i-ly, closely, without moving.
St. Ber-närd′ dog, a dog that is used to hunt for people who are lost in the snow in the Alps Mountains.
steed, a lively horse.
stū′dĭ-ō, a room where an artist works.
stū′di-ø̸us, a desire and love for study.
stûr′dy, strong.
sū′ĕt, the hard fat taken from the dead body of a cow or sheep.
sȳm′pa-thize, feel as some one else feels.

T

tärt, having a sharp, sour taste.
thăṯched, covered with a roof of straw or dry grass.
tĭm′id-ly, in a fearful manner; afraid.
tôr**ch**′es, lights made by soaking pieces of wood in something that will burn into a bright light.
tôr′tø̸ĭsø̸, a turtle.
trāil, a path through the woods.
Trĕa̸ṣ′u-ry Department, a building where a nation keeps money.

trēạt′y, promises made between two parties.

trŏp′i-cal, very warm.

trụ′ant, one who stays away from school without permission.

Tu-si-tä′la, a Samoan word meaning "Teller of Tales."

U

un-çiv′i-lized, wild and savage; coarse and rude.

un-cȯm′fort-a-ble, uneasy.

un-cŏn′scious, not knowing what is going on.

un-stĕạd′y, undecided.

V

ve-răn′dah, a house porch held up by pillars.

vĕxẹd, very much annoyed; angry.

vĭc′to-ry, defeat of an enemy.

vĭṣ′age, the face.

voy′age, journey on the sea.

W

wạm′pum, beads made of shell, used by the North American Indians as money or for making belts.

wēạv′er, one who weaves.

wee, very tiny.

wĕst′wãrd, toward the west.

whạrf, a place built on the shore of a river or other water where people may land.

whĭp-poor-wĭll′, a night bird whose cry sounds like "Whippoorwill."

wĭck′et, a small gate.

wĭst′ful, longing.

wŏȯd′pĕck-er, a bird that taps trees to find insects.

ẉrĕck, a ship destroyed at sea.

XYZ

zwĭē′bäck, slices of bread toasted dry.

251

Graph of Pupil's Weekly Silent Reading Rate

Third Grade, 19 30 Name Mary Smith

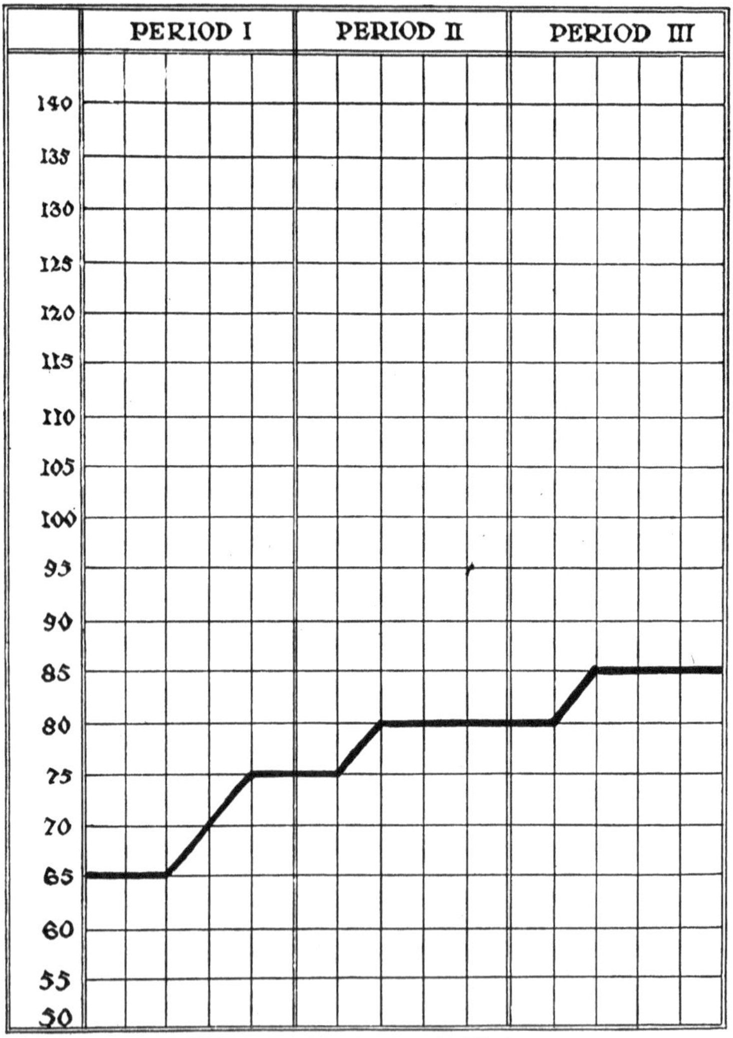

This page shows a graph filled out.

Graph of Pupil's Weekly Silent Reading Rate

Third Grade, 19___   Name _____

	PERIOD I	PERIOD II	PERIOD III
140			
135			
130			
125			
120			
115			
110			
105			
100			
95			
90			
85			
80			
75			
70			
65			
60			
55			
50			

These blank graphs provide for those who may use the book in successive years.

Graph of Pupil's Weekly Silent Reading Rate

Third Grade, 19___   Name _____

	PERIOD I	PERIOD II	PERIOD III
140			
135			
130			
125			
120			
115			
110			
105			
100			
95			
90			
85			
80			
75			
70			
65			
60			
55			
50			

These blank graphs provide for those who may use the book in successive years.

Graph of Pupil's Weekly Silent Reading Rate

Third Grade, 19___   Name _____

	PERIOD I	PERIOD II	PERIOD III
140			
135			
130			
125			
120			
115			
110			
105			
100			
95			
90			
85			
80			
75			
70			
65			
60			
55			
50			

These blank graphs provide for those who may use the book in successive years.

Graph of Pupil's Weekly Silent Reading Rate

Third Grade, 19⎯⎯ Name⎯⎯⎯⎯⎯⎯⎯⎯⎯⎯⎯⎯

	PERIOD I	PERIOD II	PERIOD III
140			
135			
130			
125			
120			
115			
110			
105			
100			
95			
90			
85			
80			
75			
70			
65			
60			
55			
50			

These blank graphs provide for those who may use the book in successive years.

We invite you to view the complete
selection of titles we publish at:
www.TEACHServices.com

scan with your mobile
device to go directly
to our website

Please write or email us your praises, reactions, or
thoughts about this or any other book we publish at:

www.TEACHServices.com ▪ (800) 367-1844

11 Quartermaster Circle
Fort Oglethorpe, GA 30742

Info@TEACHServices.com

TEACH Services, Inc., titles may be purchased in bulk
for educational, business, fund-raising, or sales
promotional use. For information, please e-mail:

BulkSales@TEACHServices.com

Finally if you are interested in seeing
your own book in print, please contact us at

publishing@TEACHServices.com

We would be happy to review your manuscript for free.

www.ingramcontent.com/pod-product-compliance
Lightning Source LLC
Chambersburg PA
CBHW070546160426
43199CB00014B/2393